Thomas Cox

A Popular History of the Grammar School of Queen Elizabeth, at

Heath, near Halifax

Thomas Cox

A Popular History of the Grammar School of Queen Elizabeth, at Heath, near Halifax

ISBN/EAN: 9783337323844

Printed in Europe, USA, Canada, Australia, Japan

Cover: Foto ©ninafisch / pixelio.de

More available books at **www.hansebooks.com**

A POPULAR HISTORY

OF

The Grammar School of Queen Elizabeth,

AT HEATH, Near HALIFAX,

BY THOMAS COX, M.A.,

MASTER OF THE SCHOOL.

" Whilest that the childe is young, let him be instructed
in vertue and lytterature ".

(Euphues, by John Lily, about 1580.)

" In tenui labor, at tenuis non gloria ".
(Virgil)

HALIFAX :
F. KING, PRINTER, EXCHANGE BUILDINGS, NORTHGATE.
1879.

To the Memory
of my School Masters,
The Right Reverend FRANCIS JEUNE, D.C.L.,
late Bishop of Péterborough:
The Right Reverend JAMES PRINCE LEE, D.D.,
late Bishop of Manchester;
and To my College Tutors,
The Reverend JOHN HYMERS, D.D.,
now Rector of Brandsburton, Yorkshire;
The Very Reverend Charles Merivale, D.D.,
now Dean of Ely,
I dedicate this little Book,
in gratitude for the many advantages which
I received from them
at School and at College.

THOMAS COX, M.A.

THE CONTENTS OF THIS BOOK.

PREFACE.

Several years ago I collected for my own information some particulars relating to the History of Heath School, from Watson's History of Halifax, The Parish Church Registers, and Documents belonging to the Governors. As a suitable time was come for putting these together in a readable form, I thought of drawing up a paper to be read at a public opening of the New Buildings. I soon found, however, additional matter to such an extent that I laid aside the notion of a temporary paper, and aspired to be the writer of a permanent book. Then I found, that, if I printed the important documents in full, I should produce something too expensive for the public, and satisfactory only to antiquarians. So I thought that by digesting the information supplied by manuscripts and books I might write a popular history, suitable to the pockets and pleasure of all who cared for the School. But I found it a more difficult task than I expected. There were conclusions to be drawn from imperfect *data*; contradictions to clear up; and often a want of continuity in the history. There had been so little interest taken in the School that scarcely anything was known of the Masters beyond their existence; and, for nearly two hundred years, there was nothing certain of the scholars which they had made. For some seventy or eighty years, even the names of the Governors were wanting; and yet, as they had property to manage, they must have signed documents, though I do not know of any. However, I have carefully gone through the Parish Church Registers, Brearcliffe's MSS.

of his own times, the Governors' Books and Documents, and the Papers which under the name of "Our Local Portfolio" appeared in the Halifax Guardian some twenty years ago. I have also gone through all the books in the Library of the Literary and Philosophical Society which I thought might possibly contribute something to the accuracy of a statement, or even a word or name, though not furnishing a paragraph or supplying a sentence. I have gone over several large volumes more than once, as names forced themselves on my notice which seemed to have no connection with my subject when I first read them. But I must beg pardon of my readers beforehand, if sometimes they find my knowledge inferior to theirs: for, twelve months ago, I was entirely ignorant of the old West Riding families, which happen to be mentioned in this book; and even now I have only such knowledge as a temporary sojourner in their land might get. I must also say, that, where I have had recourse to conjecture, I have honestly reasoned out the matter, and suspended my judgment for months, until I found statements in books to render that conjecture probable, and I have had no one to help me.

I must ask readers to bear in mind that this is a popular account of the School, and therefore documents are out of place. I have nevertheless introduced one or two, for reasons given where they occur. Nor have I gone into details about subscriptions, donations, or legacies; for they are very numerous, and very small in amount in general, and seem as forced as charity often is for the sake of appearances. I have forborne too to dwell on the fact, which surprised me in my researches, that Halifax as a town took very little interest in the School, either in promoting its foundation or in supplying it with scholars. Even when the School flourished most, it seems to have owed its success to foreigners, not natives; and its very locality near the town was accidental. Still I hope, that, if any interest in the School is aroused by the present publication, all the documents connected with it will some day be given to the world in full (either by private liberality or by public subscription); and I shall be glad to contribute to such a work all the other particulars that this History is based on.

I may add that I have generally preserved the old way of speaking of people, as for instance, John Lacy, though we may now think it too familiar; that I have spelled words as we now spell them, except there is a point in keeping the old form; and that P.R. means "Parish Registers", and L.P. "Our Local Portfolio". I have quoted very few Authorities, because they would take up too much space in a popular Work, so condensed as this.

My readers must not measure the value of the book by the price which I have put upon it; that was fixed low to induce people to buy it; and though I have not got subscribers enough to pay for its publication, I print it because I promised to do so when a certain number of copies had been subscribed for. It has cost me many hundred hours of research, to say nothing of the trouble which I have had in writing over again passages, which I thought contained all the information that could possibly be got when I first wrote them. It has however given me a great deal of pleasure, such as no reader can possibly feel: yet I have endeavoured to write for his satisfaction; and I hope he will not think that he has thrown his money away, nor that the book is smaller than he expected.

I have especially to thank Mr. S. T. Rigge for the loan of several important books; and Mr. Craven, of Clapton Lodge, and Mr. Lister, of Shibden Hall, for some communications relating to Sterne. Mr. C. J. Fox and Mr. Stopford have kindly prepared the drawings for the illustrations, and deserve

x.

thanks both from me and from the readers of the book. I
am indebted also to the Governors of the School, and to those
of the Waterhouse Charity, for kindly allowing me to search
into their documents. The Architects of the New Buildings
have also kindly contributed an account of them, and a
Photolithograph of the Front as seen from Free School Lane.

Now, I feel that I have an apology to make for the style
in which the work is written. After six months research
I thought that I had got all the information that I could
possibly get; and I tried to put it into a readable shape.
As far back as February I wrote the history of the School,
and many of the other chapters, feeling a strong dissatisfaction
with the result of my labours : but afterwards by going
over the ground again I was enabled to glean a few more
grains, and, even while the work was passing through the
press, I was enabled to clear up some doubts which detracted
from the merits of the work. The consequence was that I
had to insert words or phrases or even whole sentences, and to
alter others, so that in many places I find the flow of the style
sadly obstructed. I have likened it myself to what takes
place on a rapid stream when the ice breaks up, and huge
lumps collect here and odd masses float there to spoil the
even tenour of its current. Had I had a sufficient number
of subscribers, I would have torn the book to pieces and
re-written it; but those who have promised me their support
have unfortunately to suffer because so many whom I had
hoped to attract have kept themselves aloof from a work,
in which I nevertheless believe that they feel an interest.

I will say but a few words in conclusion. First, this
School may be called " The School of the three Queens ".
Its original Charter in 1585 was signed by Elizabeth: the
confirmation of the Charter in 1729 was signed by Caroline,
the Queen of George II., and its recent Scheme was signed
by Victoria.

Secondly, I quote from the original prospectus the sources of this History, and a statement of what I intended to give to the subscribers.

The materials made use of are collected from :—

1. The documents in the Parish Church Registers ;
2. The Registers themselves in reference to births, marriages, and burials ;
3. *Brearcliffe's MSS. on matters connected with Halifax, in the early part of the 17th century ;
4. The Sterne correspondence concerning the School from 1725 to 1730 ;
5. The various Histories of Halifax ;
6. " Our Local Portfolio," a series of papers, which appeared in the " Halifax Guardian " between 1856 and 1861 ;
7. The Minute Books of the Governors of the School. Besides these, many books relating to the History of Yorkshire have supplied items of importance.

The Book will not be encumbered with documents, but will consist of information supplied by them, or of inferences drawn from them. It will be illustrated by engravings of the old and new buildings, and some other objects of interest. It will also contain Lists of the Masters and Governors from the earliest time, and of all the pupils since 1840, and of some other earlier ones.

Thirdly, I quote a passage from the Life of a celebrated Critic, Gilbert Wakefield, which I have but recently seen, respecting the advantages of such Schools as that at Heath.

---

* This compilation, which was once in the Parish Church Library, and is now in the keeping of the Waterhouse Charity Trustees, was made by John Brearcliffe, an Apothecary in Halifax, who was the son of Edmond Brearcliffe, Parish Clerk in Dr. Favour's time. He died December 4th, 1682, aged 63. Caution is necessary in the use of the work. I have found about sixteen mistakes in those parts, with which I have had to do.

He says that it is in the Preface to Plutarch's Treatise on Education by Dr..Edwards. "I am so far from lamenting the years, which are usually passed in a Grammar School, that I consider them, *if well employed,* as the most important period of life. The peculiar exercise of the understanding, which is requisite to investigate and ascertain the precise meaning of an ancient author, is the best, if not the only method of training up the juvenile mind to form just conclusions on more momentous subjects. If, on the other hand, boys are permitted or encouraged to wander from one pursuit to another, and to remain satisfied with a superficial knowledge of each; we shall in vain look forward to those mature fruits, without which it will be impossible to establish a character".

Halifax,
Oct. 31st, 1879.

TO SUBSCRIBERS.

This Book, according to Prospectuses issued in June and July, is published in four forms, distinguished in the annexed List by the letters A., B., C., and D.

(A.)—The original Form, consisting of the History and some Illustrations, price 4s.

(B.)—A, with two Lectures attached, illustrative of the state of Education in England when the majority of our present Grammar Schools were founded, price 5s.

(C.)—A, with four Photographs of Masters and some additional Illustrations, price 6s. 6d.

(D.)—C, with the two Lectures attached, price 7s. 6d.

₊ The above prices apply only to Copies subscribed for: the remaining Copies will be supplied at a higher price, but only in the Forms C. and D; very few of the latter are left.

LIST OF SUBSCRIBERS.

Governors.	A	B	C	D		A	B	C	D
Edwards, Sir H.				1	Bamford, J.				1
Hill, J. E.				1	Bancroft, J.	1			
Hope, Rev. J.	1				Birtwhistle, Mrs.			1	
Longbottom, J. W.	1				Blackburn, Mrs.	1			
Lawson, J.	1				Bonser, J. W.	1		1	
Lawson, W. H.		·2		1	Booth, E. W.				1
Rothwell, W.	1	1	1		Brown, Rev. J. F.			1	
Swallow, J. H. .. ., ...				1	Caw, J. (Senr.)				1
Waterhouse, Major				1	Clegg, J.				1
Masters and Ex-Masters.					Crossley, Mrs.				1
Brookes, Rev. W. J.				1	Dawes, Captain	1			
Clayton, J.				1	Denison, J.			1	
Earnshaw, Rev. J. W.	1				Dewhirst, W. T.				1
Gooch, Rev. J.	1		1		Dyson, Rev. W.				1
Pitts, Rev. T.				1	Edgar, D. R.				1
Poiré, H. C.				1	Edleston, Rev. Dr.			1	
Sadd, W. E.				1	Edwards, H.				1
Whitehead, Rev. W. C.				1	Farrar, T. H.			1	
Past or Present Scholars or					Finch, Rev. T.			1	
their Parents.					Firth, W.	1			
Ainley, D.	1				Fletcher, Rev. R. C.	1			
Alexander, Dr.			1		Fox, C. J.			1	
Ashworth, Rev. J. A.	1				Francis, E.				1
Baines, F.			1		Hall, Rev. J.	1			

	A	B	C	D
Hill, A. S.				1
Holmes, Rev. C. R.			1	
Holroyde, J. B.			1	
Hoyle, G. (Senr.)				1
Hoyle, G. (Junr.)			1	
Huntriss, E.				1
Jeffery, Rev. S.			2	
Jessop, J.			1	
Kenny, C. S.		1		
Kenny, W. F.	1			
Kirk, J. M.			1	
Marshall, Rev. J.	1			
Maude, W. W.			1	
Mitchell, J.	1			
Moffett, Rev. R.			1	
Newman, E.				1
Norris, H. A.			2	
Norris, S. P.			2	
Parkinson, T.				2
Patchett, M.	1			
Rankin, M. H.			2	
Robinson, H.			1	
Robinson, R. H.				1
Rhodes, S.	5			
Rouse, J. C.	1			
Rouse, Rev. W. A.	1			
Salmond, D.	1			
Shoesmith, J.			1	
Smeeton, G. F.		1		
Snow, T. C.			1	
Stansfeld, Colonel				1
Storey, W.	1			
Swallow, R. D.			1	
Thomas, W. F.			1	
Town, Rev. B.	1			
Turner, T.				1
Waghorn, H. R.	1			
Wainhouse, J. E.	1		1	
Warneford, Rev. J. H.				2
Whitaker, W. H.	1			
Woodhead, D.			1	
Residents in Halifax or the Neighbourhood.				
Bagot, Rev. G.	1			
Barber, W. C.			1	

	A	B	C
Browne, G. B.			1
Craven, W.	1		
Clark, Mrs.	1		
Greenwood, J. H.			1
Highley, H. H.			1
Hughlings, H.			
Jackson, B. W.	1		
Leeming, Messrs.			
Leyland, F. A.	1		
Literary & Philosophical Society			
Lister, J.			3
McCrea, H. C.	1		
Mechanics' Institute	1		
Millson, Rev. F. E.			1
Perkinton, J.		1	
Prescott, Mrs.			
Rigge, S. T.	1		
Roberts, Dr.	1		
Sagar, ( )	1		
Spencer, W.			1
Stafford, R. P.			1
Thackrah, A.	1		
Thomas, J.			1
Walker, F.			1
Ward, J. W.			1
Wright, J. H.			
Subscribers residing at a distance.			
Ainsworth, T. (Blackburn)	1		
Butterton, Rev. Dr. (Rhyl)	1		
Brandt, Miss (Leamington)		1	
Brookes, Rev. T. (Wakefield)	1		
Elborne, H. (Cambridge)			
Finch, Miss (Cambridge)			
Fisher, A. (Gosport)			1
Gorst, J. E. (London)			
Heppel, G. (Weston super Mare)			1
Hopkinson, G. H. (London)	1		
Hulbert, Rev. Canon (Almondbury)	1		
Landon, Rev. J. T. B. (Ledsham)	1		
Robson, R. (London)			1
Robson, T. (Cambridge)			1
Shaw, Rev. F. (Fen Drayton)			
Shaw, Miss (Waltham)			
Weston, Rev. W. R. (Hexthorpe)			1

CHAPTER I.

SHORTLY after the beginning of the reign of Henry the Eighth, Richard Pace* the King's chief Secretary, was present, as he tells us, at a feast where there were many guests, and a conversation was carried on about the best way of educating children. A gentleman, who was present, fell into a great rage at the praise bestowed on learning. "What nonsense!", said he, "a curse on your learning! Your learned "men are all beggars. Why, Zounds, I had rather my son "were hanged than become a student! Learning be left to "peasants' sons!" Pace, who was unknown to him, with a gentle reproof told him that the King's service would require better men than fowlers and hunters; but fowling and hunting was all that many then cared for; and the King's service had to be carried on by ecclesiastics rather than laymen. But what a change had come over the country before that century came to an end! Such an effect was produced by the establishment of Grammar Schools that

---

* Richard Pace held a Prebendal Stall in York Minster in 1514, became Archdeacon of Dorset in the same year, and Dean of St. Paul's in 1519. He held several other preferments. He was a friend of the celebrated Erasmus. He wrote a work on the Advantages of Learning. It is *possible* that he is the same Richard Pace as was Rector of Barwick-in-Elmet, the resignation of which living by a Richard Pace took place in the year when Richard Pace became Dean of St. Paul's.

peasants' sons had it in their power to rise to the highest offices in Church and State, and men of birth were forced to adopt a different tone to recommend them to their Sovereign. By degrees laymen became educated, and, leaving the ecclesiastical rewards to peasants' sons, fitted themselves for civil employments†; but the learning of Grammar Schools was still useful for what were called the Three learned Professions, Divinity, Law, and Physic; and they did the country good service for many generations. At length however the supply exceeded the demand, and with the lack of competent scholars the teachers became in many instances careless, and such schools lost their repute. In 1562, the Speaker of the House of Commons in an address to the Queen took notice of the want of schools; a hundred were wanting which before that time had been; there was a decay of learning to the dishonour both of God and the commonwealth; the people were trained up and led in blindness for want of instruction, and became obstinate; he therefore advised that this should be seen to. And seen to it was, and in good earnest; but not so much by the Authorities as by local exertions. But there was a shortsightedness, though not altogether to be blamed; it was due to want of experience as to what was really needed; and zeal ran riot. The zealous founders of Grammar Schools had thought, that, being in advance of the age, the age would

---

† W. Harrison in 1577 writes of the Courtiers of Queen Elizabeth :—" There are very few of them, which have not the use and skill of sundry speeches, besides an excellent vein of writing beforetime not regarded....Truly it is a rare thing with us now, to hear of a courtier. which hath but his own language." Sir Philip Sidney, writing to his brother Robert in 1580, recommends him to read for practical use the Greek Historians Herodotus, Thucydides, Xenophon, and Diodorus, and the Roman Historians Livy and Tacitus: and " to take delight in the Mathematicals " i. e., in Mathematics, as we should now say. Robert was at this time travelling in Germany with a Tutor " Master Savell "; I wonder whether this was one of our Saviles. Sir H. Savile, fellow of Merton, was abroad in 1578, &c. Thomas Savile, his brother, was abroad about 1580.

never overtake them, and what was best for the present need
would be good for all future time. Such schools had no
power of adapting themselves to altered circumstances, and
in the long run thousands of pounds were wasted which might
have been turned to good account. Even in the reign of
James I. the celebrated Bacon thought that too many
Grammar Schools had been founded, yet their number has
been greatly increased since his time. Within the present
century (though not for peasants' sons or those of limited
means) Proprietary Schools have been established in great
numbers and on a large scale after the fashion of the old
Grammar Schools. This too is a disadvantage to the community in some respects : the good leaven of gentility, which
leavened the whole lump in days gone by, has been withdrawn,
and the comparatively poor have no example set before them
to lift them upwards, so that the gulf between class and
class widens.

Let us now look a little to the origin of Grammar Schools.
The charter of Heath School states the object of the School
to be "for the bringing up teaching and instructing of
children and youth in Grammar and other good learning".
If we refer to contemporary accounts, we find that Grammar*
was confined chiefly to elementary Latin and Greek, so far
as to enable students at the University to fit themselves for
the Trivium, or threefold course of study required for all
Graduates, which consisted of Grammar, Rhetoric, and Logic;
whence these schools were often called Trivial schools.† The

---

* Brinsley's *Ludus Literarius*, published in 1612, says "Such only should be
sent to the Universities who....in a love of learning will begin to take pains of
themselves, having attained in some sort the former parts of learning; being
good Grammarians at least, able to understand, write, and speak Latin in good
sort." "Grammar" embraced a good deal, for a Candidate for the B. A. degree
was said "to commence in Grammar."

† "It is a trivial Grammar School Text." *Bacon's Essays, XII.*

4

Quadrivium, or fourfold course, consisted of Arithmetic, Music, Geometry, and Astronomy‡. Grammar Schools then had to fit a man especially for Speaking and Reasoning, and for acquiring all knowledge that could be gained from a study of the best Classical Authors of Rome and Greece, and this was considered so essential, that Degrees in Divinity, Law, and Physic, were only granted to those who had mastered the Trivium, or had graduated in Arts, as it was termed. Next, the phrase "good learning" has to be interpreted in reference to the usage of the times. It was pure classical Literature as opposed to the Scholastic learning, which before the sixteenth century formed the basis of the University Course. We find such language as this used of the Universities: "Nothing was known there but Latin, and that in the most depraved style of the Schoolmen": "in process of time good letters were brought in, and some knowledge of the Mathematics."

In times antecedent to the Reformation Free Grammar Schools had been founded, (1) in connection with Religious Establishments, as Cathedrals and Collegiate Churches; (2) in combination with Chantries; (3) by Trade-guilds; and (4) by Individuals, whether Ecclesiastics or Laymen. After the confiscation of Ecclesiastical estates by the Crown, most of these schools were ruined; but as the country suffered in consequence, many were after the lapse of a few years brought into existence again and endowed by the Crown on petition of the inhabitants of the parish in which there had formerly been a school; others were founded by Gentlemen who had been successful in their trade or profession; and some by those whose estates had been increased by the

‡ A Poem written about 1480 says "Clerkis that the VII artez cunne," *i. e.*, Clerks that know the seven arts.

acquisition of Church lands. In the reigns of Edward, Mary, Elizabeth, a very large number of Schools received Charters by these means. The Report of the Schools Inquiry Commission mentions 63 in the reign of Henry VIII, 51 under Edward VI, 19 from Mary, and 138 from Elizabeth. But the School of Heath, near Halifax, differs in its foundation from nearly all the others throughout the country; for on enquiry it will be found that it had no endowment from the Crown, nor any private endowment from an individual or individuals, when its Charter was obtained. It is charitable to suppose that it was started in hope by its promoters; and fifteen years elapsed from the date of the Charter before a Master was appointed, so little interest did the people in general take in its foundation. The Charter makes Queen Elizabeth speak of "the humble suit made unto us by the inhabitants of the parish and vicarage of Halifax", but that seems to refer only to the twelve mentioned in it as the Governors, who were formally the inhabitants. Of these twelve, three (John Lacy of Brearley; John Savile of Bradley; and Brian Thornhill of Fixby;) are described as Esquires, one (Francis Ashburn, Vicar of Halifax) as Clerk; two (Henry Savile of Blaidroyd, and Henry Farrar of Ewood) as Gentlemen; and the remaining five (William Deane of Exley, Robert Wade of Sowerby, John Deane of Deanehouse, Anthony Hirst of Greetland, George Firth of Firthhouse, and John Hanson of Woodhouse,) as Yeomen. Not one of these besides the Vicar resided in the Township of Halifax, and some of them four or five miles off; nor do we know that more than three were ever connected with a University, the Vicar and the two Saviles. It would be interesting to know what suggested the idea of a Grammar School to them, and who was the prime mover in realising it.

But it seems to me that the origin of the School was due to the Savile family.* Several of them had been or were at the time members of the University of Oxford, and two at least distinguished themselves in learning. Several of the first Governors, as Lacy, Thornhill, Hanson, were connected with the Saviles by marriage; Ashburn, Farrer, and John Deane, had married into the Lacy family; three others are mentioned as executors in wills in connection with the Hansons and Saviles. The connection of the Governors then with the Saviles seems very clear. If we look at their places of abode, we find Lacy, Hanson, Thornhill, William Deane, Hirst, and Firth, residing in the neighbourhood of John Savile, and John Deane and Wade close neighbours of Farrer. These may be said to represent the valley of the Calder, and were away from the town of Halifax, Ashburn alone seeming to represent Halifax, and he not connected with it by birth.†

---

* "Since your father's time (Sir John Savile) no man hath done so much in the School affairs as myself" says Dr. Favour in 1618, to Sir H. Savile. (L.P. No. LIII.)

† An examination of the names of the principal subscribers in both of Dr. Favour's Subscription Lists points to the same conclusion. See Chap. XIV, §1, and Chap. XVI.

CHAPTER II.

THE FOUNDATION OF HEATH SCHOOL.

A S to the time when the promoters of the School determined to apply for a Charter, we know nothing. John Savile was at Oxford in 1561, and some time after: he then became a barrister, residing for the most part at the Temple in London, and not spending much time in Yorkshire. He could pay but little attention to the matter. The petition for the Charter was probably laid before the Queen by the Earl of Shrewsbury, as he was closely connected with the Saviles, and such petitions were generally presented through a Nobleman at Court. It was favourably received, and a Charter was granted and signed in February, 1584-5. Henry Farrer paid all the expenses incurred, which was no doubt a pretty good sum : but he could perhaps better afford it than the other Governors, as he had a few years before obtained the manor of Midgley by his marriage with the daughter of John Lacy. At any rate it was a generous act on his part, but I wonder who thanked him for it?

Yet all seemed in vain. The newly formed Corporation had no revenues or possessions to be* Governors of, and nobody stirred to give effect to the Charter. John Savile, as I have said, seemed most concerned in the foundation of the School, but he was seldom at his house, Bradley in

---

* We must remember that Governors were so called as Trustees of the Property, and not as managers of the details of the Schools. See, for an instance, the Deed in Chap. XVI.

Stainland, being engaged in London by his official duties as Barrister and Judge, or with the Council of the North at York. John Lacy and Vicar Ashburn died within a few months after the Charter was signed. There seemed no anxiety on the part of the people that were to be benefited by it. Nobody came forward to urge the Governors to make the School a reality. It existed only in parchment. Those that were children and youth when the Charter was obtained became men before anything further was done. Farrer had paid his money for nothing. The hopes at first entertained seemed never to be realised, and Halifax sent none of her poor men's sons to either University. The decaying great families of the neighbourhood, who sought to acquire the means of living by positions in Church or State, when their estates got less by division or by sale, were however well represented at Oxford at the end of the 16th century and the beginning of the 17th. The Saviles, the Drakes, the Clays, the Ramsdens, the Deanes, the Waterhouses, the Wilkinsons of Elland, and others were distinguished at the Universities, principally at Oxford; but they were able to support themselves during the necessary education. But nobody lent a helping hand in turning to a good account the ability which God had given the tradesman's or peasant's son. It was not till 1593 that an advocate raised a voice on their behalf, and he a stranger to the place by birth or marriage, the celebrated Dr. Favour, Vicar of Halifax. He had been educated at the then most famous School in England, Winchester College, and had become a Scholar and Fellow of New College, Oxford, which William of Wykeham had established for those who had profited most by his Winchester foundation. Dr. Favour naturally wished that the Halifax boys should have an opportunity of getting a University education as far as they were fit for it. After he was settled

in his Vicarage and had time to look about him, he set to the
work with his usual energy. He found a Charter for a School
and a few Governors without anything to govern. There was
no property given, no Master, no School-house. Of the
original Governors several had died, one spent his time
principally in London, and others lived some four or five
miles off. Some ten years had elapsed since the Charter
had been petitioned for, and we may imagine the indifference
which the survivors would feel, when they had seen the
nonfulfilment of their early hopes. The places of those who had
died had been filled up by successors to keep the Corporation
in existence, but they had not felt the interest in the matter
which was once felt when John Savile was an active man
among them, so that owing to their neglect there were only
three properly qualified Governors in existence in 1607, and
application had to be made to the Archbishop of York to
fill up the vacancies before any valid act could be done. For
ten years before this Dr. Favour had bestirred himself to get
the School established, though he does not seem to have
been legally a Governor himself until the end of 1607. He
seems to have considered it part of his duty as Vicar of
Halifax: he fought hardly for the rights of " the poor School
and the poor people," as he at a later period calls those
who had been deprived of their dues by mismanagement both
in this respect and in others. He had enlisted Sir John
Savile on his side, and a great deal of correspondence passed
between the two on the subject of the School.

It is singular that such a state of things should have
existed. We can only imagine that the Charter was carefully
locked up somewhere, and the Governors were never informed
of its terms. Else how could so many elected Governors
have never qualified? and how was it that the defect was
not found out for so many years?

It was not until the beginning of 1597 that anything definite could be done. In February of that year the Governors got possession of two acres of land given by the Farrers of Ewood, a corporate seal* was provided, and steps were taken to get up a subscription for erecting a suitable building. Some arrangement seems to have been made for this purpose between Sir John Savile and Dr. Favour on a visit of the former to his country-house. An appeal in writing,† dated Halifax, July 16th, was made by a letter signed (not by the Governing body but) by "Your loving friends Jn. Savile and John Favour" to some Gentlemen of the neighbourhood, intimating that unless the School were "erected within a certain time" it would lose certain possessions conditionally promised, and asking them to set down the sum they would bestow towards so charitable an action, as it was intended the work should begin immediately after Sep. 20. An agreement was made by Dr. Favour with a builder of Hipperholme, named Martin‡ Akroyd, a free-mason, and particulars were sent with a plan to Sir John in London. The builder was to receive £120 together with the materials of an old house which stood on the ground

---

* I draw this inference from the date on the present seal; but see Chap. III. §1.

† The letters to be found in L. P. Nos. CXLIX. and CL.

‡ In the Parish Registers under Nov. 8, 1591, his marriage with Sara Ramsden occurs and under March 20, 1617 (i. e. 1618 N. S.) his burial.

It is curious to find his name spelled differently in the same letter. Altogether there are found seven different forms of it: Akroyd, Akroyed, Acroid, Acroyd, Acroyde, Ackeroyd, Eaycroyd. Such was the disregard of spelling in those times. Martin, Abraham, and John, are mentioned in various documents. Whether they were brothers or the Christian name of the builder was not accurately known, does not appear. Wm. Ackroyd who founded a Scholarship in 1517, has his name spelled Aikeroide, Akeroide, Akerode, Akeroyde, in one and the same document, and outside it Aykroyde, Aikroyde, (L. P. CLXIII); in another Ackroyd; in another Acroyde, Acroide, Acrode. A member of the builder's family (perhaps) appears in the Waterhouse Charity's Accounts: "1651 Paid Akeroyde for the Hospitall house 5s."

and such timber as should be voluntarily given. Dr. Favour asked Sir John's advice about the means of assuring the money to the workmen, about making the collections, and for his good help in general that the work might "be done with reasonable beauty and comeliness." This was on Sep. 29th, and the agreement with the builder, if satisfactory to Sir John, was to be concluded about the middle of October.

We hear nothing more of the School until the following summer, so that some unexpected difficulty had probably arisen; indeed there was afterwards a good cause of complaint, for men who had promised subscriptions hung back, as the Doctor says, not wishing to subscribe unless they saw others do so, and even expecting the liberality of "other towns" to make up their deficiency. He persevered, however, determined not to be beaten in so good a cause : he pressed it on his neighbours in public and in private; he wrote to every township with his own hand, and sent collectors round to make sure of the slow. At last, on Thursday in Whit- sunweek, June 8th, 1598, after the sermon on the usual Lectureday, he went (as he says) "with all his clergy and some other neighbours, and consecrated the ground with a short prayer and a psalm......and committed the blessing of the work to God." But his satisfaction on seeing the favourable progress of his good work was damped by the fact of a smaller attendance than he had expected. No doubt he often visited the spot afterwards, but from some cause or other the workmen were dilatory: he longed for the presence of Sir John to stir them up, but he did not come; and we find that the building was not finished in the time agreed on, so that Sir John at last refused to give the builder his full pay. Among the debts owing to his estate in 1617, his Executors mention £13 10s. as due from Sir John Savile, perhaps on this very account.

12

But what were the other Governors doing all the while? Did they appoint none of their body to look after the progress of the work and keep the builder to his duty? None, alas! is mentioned as feeling any interest in the work either then or afterwards; and the Doctor is obliged after the lapse of some twenty years to say in self-defence that he had himself procured almost all the revenues of the School, and that some of the Governors had never been present at the meetings though he had sent for them.

But to go back to 1598. About two months after the foundation of the School was laid, Gilbert, Earl of Shrewsbury,* Edward Savile, Esq., and Sir George Savile, gave six acres of "weak, stony, and bruery land†" with "a house called a Schole-house‡ lately built," altogether " of the annual value of eightpence " (!), to the Governors of the School, which they obtained possession of in the following January, 1598-9.

---

* In 1515 the then Earl of Shrewsbury was guardian of Henry Savile of Thornhill. His son Edward Savile (who was supposed to be weak of intellect) afterwards put himself under the protection of the Talbots, and his family tried to get him out of their hands. Sir Henry willed the bulk of his property away from Edward to the Lupset branch of the family, which was represented by Sir George, who afterwards married Mary, the daughter of George, and sister of Gilbert, Earls of Shrewsbury. It was consequently through the Saviles that the Earl of Shrewsbury had any connection with the School, so that the land given probably formed part of the estate of Sir Henry Savile.

† *terræ debilis lapidosæ et brueræ.*" This is alluded to in the Inscription over the School-house door. *Bruera*, a corruption of an older form *brugaria* (French, *bruyére*), which was used for "heather" in the Middle Ages, is defined in Dictionaries of Medieval Latin as " *Ager sterilis, vepribus et dumetis horridus,*" *i. e.*, *barren land, horrid with brambles and thickets.* I quote this, as illustrating the Inscription.

‡ In Brearcliffe's MSS. this is called "Scale-house." It was probably a rude erection, a sort of permanent hut, which was very common in former times. In many places in the West Riding and in Lancashire there are houses still called "Scholes" or "Scale-house." So that we are not to suppose that the School was given with the land. The School in fact seems to have been built on the Farrers' gift.

13

There seems to have been a small addition made to this
a few years afterwards* ; so that on the whole there
were about eleven acres of land for the support of the
School. All this however required a great deal to be done
to it before it became profitable. For several years "plowing
and hacking and manureing " were gradually carried on, as
we find it stated in an old document. And there seems to
have been no provision for any other stipend for a Master.
Dr. Favour found only a Charter when he began; and now
after the lapse of several years there is nothing further
than a School and a few acres of stony land. But in 1600
he got a Master, a Graduate of a local family perhaps, who
had energy and patriotism enough to work for the good cause
with a soul above filthy lucre. In August 1600, one Richard
Wilkinson, Bachelor of Arts, was elected Master, and in a
few days was presented to the Archbishop of York for
admission to the office, according to the provisions of the
Charter. A copy of the formal document, which was written
in Latin, and (no doubt) by Dr. Favour, is still preserved
in the Parish Registers. It is dated from Bradley, the seat
of Sir John Savile. A copy of it will be found in Chap. X,
under " Mr. Wilkinson".

---

* Brearcliffe tells us of a lease of lands granted to the Governors in 1602 from the
Governors of Sedbergh School, which was liberally endowed by William Harrison.

CHAPTER III.

§1. THE SCHOOL SEAL.   §2. INSCRIPTION ON THE HOUSE.
§3. STIPEND OF THE MASTER OF A GRAMMAR SCHOOL.
§4. SUBSCRIPTIONS TO THE ORIGINAL SCHOOL.

THE School being now established, we will stop for a few moments to consider some points of interest connected with the School before we proceed with our History.

§1. The corporate body had a common seal. I had always thought that the present seal was the one which had been in use from the beginning, but Brearcliffe gives a description of the only seal which he knew, thus:—"Ther is a free schoole seale in an ovall form with Sigil: Scholam R: Eliz: vicar Fav: Hallifax writt about it and in ye midst [*some words in cipher**] letter writt in it a rose at Top and p'cullis at bottom." I append a copy of the present seal, so that the difference is seen at once. There is no record of the time when an alteration was made, but it was probably made because of the introduction of the word "Fav:" in it. The rose and portcullis are the badges of the Tudor family. The legend "Qui mihi discipulus puer es cupis atque," consists of part of the first line of an exhortation† to youths in Lily's Latin Grammar. This is written in Latin Elegiac verse, and the first two lines are

---

* Possibly, "form of a book ['book' is certain] or."—I cannot help thinking that Brearcliffe'has made some mistake. His MSS. is hurriedly and badly written here. Not being very well acquainted with Latin, he has written Scholam for Schol. and left out Gram. He also read VICARIAT. as VICAR IAT. and then changed I into F. The final letter is so written that it may be taken either for t or v; but F is clear and bold. The legend on the seal is sigillum liberæ grammaticalis scholæ reginæ Elizabethæ vicariatus Halifaxensis, i. e., the seal of the free grammar school of Queen Elizabeth, of the vicarage of Halifax.

† This is entitled "Guilielmi Lilii ad suos discipulos monita Pædagogica; seu carmen de Moribus."

Qui mihi discipulus, Puer, es, cupis atque doceri,
Huc ades, haec animo concipe dicta tuo.
(Thou who art my pupil, boy, and desirest to be taught,
come here, grasp these sayings with thy mind.)
§2. Over the entrance to the present School-house is a
stone, which was probably removed from the old house,
containing the following Inscription:—

In Favorem Reipvbl.

Terra mala et sterilis dvmetis obsita, saxis
Horrida, que nvllis invēta est frvgib' apta,
Sed bona gens popvlvs sāct', pietatis et ardens
Relligionis opvs tantū prodvxit, vt inde
Terra bona et possit bona gens benedicier ecᶜᵉ
Sic dnī terrā dominos non terra beavit.
Elizabetha div vivat, qvae talia nobis
Indvlsit monimēta. Devs sic svmē secvdes
Hoc opvs vt vigeat, perq' ōnia saecvla dvret.
Sic nos Christe, tvo sic nostra dicam' honori.

Jacta svnt Fvndam 8º Jvnii Aº Dnī 1598:
Elizab. Reginae 40.

This may be expressed in English as follows:—
For the Favour* of the Country.

The land was bad and barren all, with thickets overgrown;
Not fit for crops of any kind, but rough with horrid stone;
Then people warm with piety, and holy in their thought,
This greatest of religious works into existence brought,
To make the land of greatest good and bless the people too:
And so a blessing to the land, not to the owners grew;
Long time the Queen Elizabeth, who granted us such grace;
And prosper Thou, O God, this work, that it may never cease,
But live in vigour through all time. So, Christ, with this intent,
We give ourselves, we give our means, unto Thine honour bent.

The Foundations were laid June 8th, A.D. 1598,
In the fortieth year of Queen Elizabeth.

---

* I have put "Favour" when "Benefit" would better suit the sense, because
I think that the Doctor, who composed the verses, had a love of his own name.
It seems also to nave been on the School Seal, if Brearcliffe is right in his
statement. In the presentation too of Richard Wilkinson to the Abp. he goes
out of his way to pray His Grace to admit him to the office of Schoolmaster
"cum favore", with favour. See Chap. X.

§3. In the latter half of the 16th century, the usual stipend of the Master of a School was 20 marks *i. e.*, £13 6s. 8d., and that of the Usher 10 marks, besides a residence for each. We find these sums fixed in many Grammar Schools, and paid out of the Endowment. The liberality of the Founder of Harrow assigned 40 marks for the Master; and even in the reign of Henry VIII as much as £20 and a house was to be set apart for the Master of the Cathedral School at Exeter. In reducing this to the present standard we should have to multiply by a much larger sum than in the former case. If 10 or 12 were the multiplier in Henry's reign, it would be 6 or 8 towards the end of Elizabeth's. But authorities differ. The income of a Master then in 1600 might, if referred to the present value, be about £100 a year. That is small, no doubt, but we must remember that people then had to confine themselves to the bare necessaries of life. Now the poorest housekeeper has comforts unknown to a superior class in 1600. £40 was considered a good stipend for a University Professor by Henry VIII. Cooper in his "Annals of Cambridge" mentions an Act of Parliament in 1650, proposing an increase to the stipends of Masters of Colleges; from which we learn that the stipend proposed was from £120 to £150 per annum, which was in many cases double the sum enjoyed before. Small as was the usual stipend of Masters of Schools, the poor Master of Heath School was to live on hope of getting something (and that not fixed) as subscriptions came in. In a curious document in No. LV. of "Our Local Portfolio," we find that the Master received for several years from Dr. Favour the sum of £3 ! It was, subsequent to 1607, considerably increased, so that he and the Usher got more than £20 between them. But even in 1720 the whole income of the School was under £40. It was not until 1773 that the

pupil of his, who in 1637 at 13 years* of age was qualified
to enter the University of Cambridge; and John Milner too
(afterwards Vicar of Leeds and a celebrated writer) in 1642
at 14 years of age entered the same University. Samuel
Stancliffe also, of St. John's College, Cambridge, was at this
School about the same time : he valued the School so highly
that he bequeathed, in 1705, £100 for " improving and
adorning " it, as a tablet still in the School testifies. The
name of Cockman is so unusual that I should like to connect
with our Master Thomas Cockman, who graduated M.A. at
Oxford in 1697 and became Master of University College,
a College with which I can find nearly Twenty Yorkshiremen
connected in this century. If so, he would be his grandson
probably.

The good work done by the School attracted the attention
of the Vicar, Henry Ramsden ; and finding the endowment
unsatisfactory, he made a collection in 1635 for the purchase
of lands. There is a list in the Parish Registers of sums
given (1) " by such as live out of the Vicarage," (2) " by the
Governors of the said School," and (3) "by the various
townships ; " these are respectively £31, £41 6s. 8d., and
nearly £125. In the first Mr. Greenwood, Vicar of Thornhill,
gives £20, leaving £11 for three other subscribers; Eight
Governors make up the second list. Sixty-three subscribers
of the Township of Halifax are required for about £36 ;
and a corresponding number of small subscribers make up
the remainder. There are only two of these who exceed
£2, viz., Rev. Robert Booth of Sowerby Bridge, and Mr.
James Oates of Southowram.

---

* Edmund Spenser went to Cambridge when 16. The celebrated Lord Fairfax
went there before he was 16. Chief-Justice Scroggs went to Oxford in 1639 at
the age of 16.

Out of this sum the Vicar had to pay for "rebuilding the
School-chimney" and for "the boarding of the school where
the boards were wanting and defective," no large sum indeed,
but enough to shew that work was scamped even in those days.

In 1631 the plague raged violently in Heptonstall and
Ovenden, and alarm was felt in Skircoat, for we find in a
letter dated 18 July, 1631, "The fear of infection hath
driven many from School." It seems to have been written
to some Governor asking advice, but the writer's name is
not mentioned. However, Halifax and Skircoat fortunately
escaped, and the work of the School was not much interfered
with.

According to Watson one Marsh (not mentioned at all
by Wright) was "Master in 1649 according to a book*
belonging to the Waterhouse Trustees." But he must remain
among "the mute inglorious" ones. In the year 1651
one Paul Greenwood† was appointed to the Mastership. To
what family he belonged, we do not know; but there were
many Greenwoods who adapted themselves to the new state
of things. A Paul Greenwood, Gent., is on the Commission
for Pious Uses in 1651; a Daniel, Principal of Brasenose
College, Oxford, about the same time; and another Daniel,
his nephew, transferred from Christ's College, Cambridge,
to a cozy fellowship under his Uncle and in a few years to
a College Living, marrying one Mary Firth of Sowerby.
He found no difficulty in adapting himself again after the
Restoration, and so died a Parish Priest, in 1679. Our

---

* Since writing the above, I have found the book, and the entry. It is as I
conjectured, among the payments made to the Master of the School and the
Curates of the twelve old Chapelries. It stands thus :—

"Paid to Mr. March the Mayster of the freskoll 2. 0. 0". It is evidently not
Marsh. A careful scrutiny of the handwriting has convinced me that it is March.
Under the payments of 1650, however, the name is written Marshe.

† He receives his first payment from the Waterhouse Charity, Dec. 24th, 1651.

Master seems to have been equally flexible; for he held the Curacy of Illingworth from 1658 to 1666, in which-year he became Vicar of Dewsbury. From his days until the beginning of the next century we hear nothing of scholars: we only know that there were masters: even the Lists of Governors are wanting.

For want of information about the School, the following curious documents in the Parish Registers, in which the Master is concerned, may open the reader's eyes to a state of things unknown to him.

"Mr. Paule Greenwood clerke Mr. of ye ffreeschoole in Skircoate & Judith Newton of Hallifax spinster was published in ye publique meetinge place called Hallifax Church att y^c close of ye mourninge Exercise upon 3 Lords dayes (to witt) ye 28 & 30 of Aprill & ye 7 of May 1654."

"The marriage betweene y^c above named Paule Greenwood aged [a blot]* yeare & ye said Judith Newton aged XIX was solempnised before Sir John Savill Knight barr^t one of ye justices of ye peace for ye west riding in ye County of Yorke in y^c presence of Anthony Westerman & Thomas Rigge, two credible witnesses according to y^c form of ye Statute in y^t case made & p'uided the eight day of May 1654."

His first child, prematurely born, was buried before the year expired. In 1658, 1661, & 1664 he had other children baptised. This is all we know of him.

He was succeeded by John Doughty, equally unknown to fame, who was, possibly, the same as graduated B.A., 1663, and M.A., 1667, at Cambridge, being a member of Caius College. He buried a child in 1668 within a fortnight after its Baptism, and his wife in a few months afterwards. He himself was buried on Oct. 14th, 1688.

---

* Seemingly X●V (i.e., XXV.)

His successor was Thomas Lister, M.B., of Jesus College, Cambridge. It is somewhat curious that a graduate in Medicine should have sought such a post, and that the Governors should have chosen such a graduate. There was probably a good deal of laxity at the time. We know for certain nothing about him. He held the post for nearly 40 years, but for several years before his death he was superannuated, and the School was in a deplorable condition: there was an Usher in 1727 of only "about 19 or 20" years of age, who had the sole charge of the School, but was "far from being capable of discharging his duty." The Master died April 1728.* The Governors were recommended by the Archbishop "to hire a Schoolmaster by the week or month till the Charter was confirmed†;" but a year later they say in a letter to his Grace's Secretary :—"at present I question whether there be any [scholars] but what the Usher can learn who for two or three years before the old Master died took care of them." A letter dated March 14th, 1728, (i. e., at the end of 1728, or, according to our reckoning, in 1729,) was written by a lawyer of Halifax to one of the tenants of the School, in which he says:—"The country suffers basely for want of a good Master at the School, where there hath not been a Master rightly qualified for nigh 40 years last past, and if the Trustees and the Bishop had any concern for the public good since the old little good for naught fellow died, they have had time enough to have placed a good Master in the School, but there is only now a few petty scholars taught there by a young lad." Mr. Lister had evidently given little satisfaction. Now it is said that the famous Laurence Sterne was a pupil here from 1724 to 1730. He tells us in

---

* A letter from Richard Sterne to Vicar Burton, dated Nov. 7th, 1727, speaks of the Scholars having to their great loss for many years been neglected.

† See the next Chapter.

his Memoirs that his father fixed him at School near Halifax
"with an *able* Master": he wrote these Memoirs just before
his death; but in his Tristram Shandy, published some ten
years previously, he gives an account of a pedagogue such
as his hero's father would not have for his son. As most
of his characters seem drawn from the life either for praise
or blame, some schoolmaster that he had known, probably sat
for this pedagogue's portrait. If so, the original must have
been anything but suitable for the office which he held,
notwithstanding his ability. I refer my readers to Chapter
XIII for fuller particulars. During Mr. Lister's Mastership, in 1705, Samuel Stancliffe, an old pupil under Mr.
Cockman, died, leaving £100 for "improving and adorning"
the School. We do not know how it was spent. At any rate
the Governors put up an expensive Tablet in the School to
commemorate the Donor, but it is to be hoped that the
expenses were not defrayed out of the bequest. It was
probably not erected till sometime afterwards, as there was
but one Governor for many years, and the Trust had very
nearly come to an end. The sad state of things then in
existence will require our attention for a little time, for there
was in 1728 no Master to teach, and no one to receive the
rents of the School, and the Charter narrowly escaped being
forfeited. We will so far. anticipate the good that was
evolved out of the evil, as to give a copy of the Tablet
and its inscription, hoping that there may be yet some good
benefactor to follow such a noble example as that afforded
by Stancliffe*, and do for the scholars what he did for
the School.

* "The Stancliffes were an ancient family in Shibden-dale: they took their
name Stank-cliffe from an ancient stank (stagnum) at the foot of a cliff, probably
that now called the Scout." "John Stanckcliffe (aged 26) married Phebe Lum
(aged 24) in June 1657: she died March 1678." L. P. XCV. Was this a brother
of Samuel?

30

The inscription on the Tablet is:—

In Memory of the *Reverend*
Mr. SAMUEL STANCLIFFE
descended of the Ancient Family
of Scarcliffe (vere *Stancliffe*
of *Scowte*) in the west Riding of
this County of *York*, sometime of
St. Johns Colledge in *Cambridge*
& *Minister* of *Stanmore Magna*
in ye County of *Midd:* who departed
this life Decem: ye 12th An: Dom: 1705
Aged 75 years.*
By his last will bequeathed 100lb
for the improving and adorning
this *free Schoole* where he was
Educated.

1630-1 Feb. 23 (B) Samuell John Stancliffe South: (P.R.)
The large bell at the Parish Church has on it the name Stancliffe, 1691, and
was probably the gift of this family.

ry of the Reverend
Mr. STANCLIFFE
of the Antient Family
of the [vere Stancliffe
in the west Riding of
of York, Sometime of
Colledge in Cambridge
of Stanmore Mugha
Midd, who departed
...Doni 1705
...th ...ill 100.
...wll... Morning
...Schole where he was
...it ...ed...

CHAPTER VII.

THE CONFIRMATION OF THE CHARTER.

IN the year 1719 a commission was appointed to enquire into the mismanagement of a chartered Corporation* which had existed for more than three quarters of a century in connection with the Relief of the Poor. The result of it was that the members had to pay expenses and to make up all deficiencies. Exception was taken to this decision, and a new Commission was appointed, but their decision also was unfavourable. Mr. Henry Gream who was the only surviving member in 1723 transferred his office to others including Vicar Burton†. In 1724 these Gentlemen exercised powers under the old Patent, though the commissioners had declared the necessity of getting a renewal of the Patent. Now Simon Sterne, J.P., of Woodhouse, and Samuel Lister, one of the Shibden Hall Listers, had been Governors of the old Corporation, and were of course liable for their share of the expenses. Richard Sterne, J.P., as his father's heir, and husband of the widow of Mr. Lister, had two shares to pay. Naturally indignant at this, and smarting under the

---

* It owed its origin to Nathaniel Waterhouse's gift of a Workhouse for the poor in 1635, and the necessity of having magistrates to carry out the Laws for Relief of the Poor.

† The Greams (name spelled Gream, Greama, Græme; the family probably from Cumberland) lived at Heath, Shaw-Hill, and Exley, the latter estate being bought of the Deanes by Henry.—They subsequently acquired the Manor of Southowram.

loss, he looked out for some means of gratifying a spiteful
disposition, which was unfortunately a failing in the Sterne
family*. He soon finds out a flaw in the proceedings of the
new Governors: he indicts them for illegal conduct and gets
them arrested; they were liberated only under heavy bail;
the case was removed from the West Riding to Westminster;
the defendants were condemned, and had to pay all the
costs of the action. But Richard Sterne was not satisfied:
there was still a grievance to be redressed, in which he could
annoy the old Vicar. He found Heath School in very low
water; all the writings connected with it were kept at the
Vicarage, and he could not get them. We can imagine him
working on the sole Governor of the School, Henry Greamt,
who had had to suffer in 1719 for his connection with the
old Corporation, and getting him to help in making further
difficulties for the Vicar. He does not seem to know much
of the School, or of its Government, if we may judge from
his letters; but, with Greann on his side and some others,
(who suspiciously have the same names as those against
whom the original commission was issued,) he opens a communication with the Archbishop of York, who was Visitor
of the School, and gets him interested in the case. The first
step was to fill up the vacancies in the Governing body,
which were so numerous that it became a question whether
the Corporation of the School was not dissolved. For some
time before 1713 there were but eight Governors, and as
the other four were not elected at the proper time, the then
Archbishop (Dr. John Sharpe) filled up the vacancies according
to the provisions of the Charter. Mr. Burton, who became

---

* Of R. Sterne, his uncle, Thoresby says "not so hot as I feared, being the
Archbishop's son". *Diary* i, p.154.

† He had been connected with the old Corporation since 1700, and was now
probably advanced in years.

Master's income reached £50, and even then rent had to be paid for the House and Land. So poverty-stricken was the place!

§4. In the Parish Registers and the Brearcliffe MSS. there are Lists of the subscriptions and legacies which the School received during the first 50 years of its existence. They are very numerous, but out of place in a popular work like this, as they would occupy many pages. There were about 16 oaks given by the Saviles, Thornhills, and Lacys, at the building of the School, about £205 collected by Dr. Favour, and about £195 by Dr. Henry Ramsden in 1635. The legacies were small, with the exception of Brian Crowther's, which was about £300.* It was very singular that the Saviles gave no exhibitions or scholarships for youths going to the University, and that Charles Greenwood, Vicar of Thornhill, gave only £20 to Ramsden's Collection, preferring to found another School at Heptonstall, and to leave the bulk of his money to University College,† Oxford, for the benefit of Yorkshire in general. The free education at Heath School was consequently useless to poor men's sons, as a preparation for the University.

---

* Hipperholme School was better off than that at Heath, for it had a Legacy of £500.

† University College was a favorite College with the South Western parts of Yorkshire in the beginning of the seventeenth century. It had several Fellowships and Scholarships, founded by Yorkshiremen for the benefit of natives of those parts.

CHAPTER IV.

LET us now return to the School itself. In 1600 Richard Wilkinson was Master. But the land was yet unfenced, and the house wanted much to make it habitable. So the Doctor had to play the beggar again. At the end of the year he sent a letter subscribed with Sir John's name and his own to the Incumbents of the twelve Chapelries; they were requested to publish it in their Chapels, and to make a collection "among the richest and best able persons"; and, to induce people to contribute, they were to set down the names of the givers with the sums given, that they might be registered and kept in memory. (Happy thought! and they are to be seen to the present day in the Parish Registers.) The collection was to be brought to the Free School on a day to be fixed. The plan was so far successful as to bring in nearly £150, so that the new year 1601—(the year then began March 25th)—had a joyful beginning. The fences were now got up, suitable out-houses were built, proper school furniture was obtained, and "the good work" was on the road "to be speedily brought to absolute perfection." We know nothing however of the time when the Master began his work, nor of the scholars who came to him. For some cause or other the post soon became vacant. Mr. Wilkinson passes away without a sign. Whether he got better preferment or pined away we do not know. There is no trace however

of the latter in the Parish Registers; and it is to be hoped
that he fared better somewhere else, either as Schoolmaster
or as Parish Priest. But in 1603 Robert Byrron appears as
the Schoolmaster, and not long after his appointment Dr.
Favour "bestowed on the School a fair Couper's Dictionary,
and a fair Greek Lexicon, and procured a fair English Bible
in the largest volume, for reading some chapters at [the]
ordinary prayers morning and evening." He values these
books at £3 6s. 8d., which would perhaps be equivalent to
some £20 of our time. These Dictionaries (Couper's Latin,
and Scapula's Greek) are still in existence at the ˙School,
in good condition as if very little used, except that the title-
pages and many of the first leaves are wanting. The Bible
is gone. In fact, being of a Translation older than the
present, it would soon become superannuated. It might
possibly be the one, which now graces the shelves of the
Literary and Philosophical Library.

Byrron had hopes of a comfortable life, for on October
16th, 1604, he took as a helpmeet Grace Deane; and he
continued at his post until 1629, being buried on April 28th,
according to the Parish Register. He is there mentioned
as "publicae scholae Gramāticalis secundus a fundatione
magister"; language that shews also the departure of his
Patron, who entered him, when married, as "*Informator*,"
as he had styled his predecessor in his presentation to the
Archbishop. I suppose Byrron was a reading man, for he
gave to the Parish Church Library (according to Brearcliffe)
two books, "Aretinus Felinus* on the Psalms" and "Thomas
Aquinas on the Evangelists." He and the Usher taught
the Doctor's children; they were paid by him "very bounti-
fully," as he tells us, so that they were perhaps regarded as
private pupils. This is all we know of both Master and pupils.

---

* This was a name adopted by Martin Bucer.

20

But an event of importance to the School and a blessing to him and his partner happened at the end of 1607, or (as we should rather say) the beginning of 1608. Bryan Crowther, a wealthy Clothier of Halifax, who had been one of the Churchwardens in the first year of Dr. Favour's vicariate, and who, being childless, was probably worthy of the Vicar's cultivation, dies and leaves £300 for the benefit of the School.* He was buried on Jan. 12th, 1607-8, and the Doctor lost no time in securing the money. Brearcliffe tells us that there were then only three surviving governors, Farrer, Firth, and Hanson, and they wrote a letter on Jan. 15th to " my lord grace of York " about electing new Governors. Although vacancies, as we have seen, had been filled up, and Dr. Favour and several others had been reputed Governors, the terms of the Charter had not been complied with, and a difficulty was found when the Governors had to deal with property. There is a significant entry in the Parish Registers. " The 18th day of January 1607, the Governors met and assembled together at the said School and made †then and there an election of Sir Henry Savile...Daniel Foxcroft.....Antony Wade.....Isaac Waterhouse....by the full consent and agreement of us the Governors of the said School, whom we nominate and appoint as Governors by these presents." " Signed Jo: Favour, Richard Sunderland, Robert Deane." It is singular that the three surviving Governors do not sign. The arrangement made was satisfactory to the Archbishop, whose confirmation is dated Jan. 26th, 1607. Brearcliffe also tells us that Favour,

---

* John Hanson, one of the Original Governors says in a Letter to Dr. Favour in 1615 :—" You know that annuity is the fairest flower in that garden....Brian Crowdr. had a good intention (partly by your direction) to further the revenues of the School."

† Notice the determined character of the phrase.

21

Sunderland, Wade, and Waterhouse, took their Corporal
Oaths to do and execute their office well and truly on
Feb. 12th, 1607*. Thus the legacy was secured, and could
be legally dealt with: and its proceeds were added to the
stipends of the Master and Usher, as Byrron tells us.

In 1611 a demand had to be made on Thomas Thornhill
for the arrears of a Rent-charge left by Bryan Thornhill.
The Governors wish to make him a Fellow-Governor, but
they want him first to pay up the arrears due and to promise
future payment.—He promises and is elected: but in 1624
there were twelve years of arrears, and a Chancery suit
had to enforce payment†.

In 1618 the Vicar had to defend himself against false
statements made to Sir H. Savile by one Robert Lawe,
respecting the way in which he had dealt with Crowther's
bequest. He wrote a warm letter in self-defence, in which
we hope he was successful. It is given in L. P. No. LIII.

---

* He writes 1617, but that is evidently an error.
† Brearcliffe says, " 10ᵗᵇ spent in Mr. Thornhill suite ".

CHAPTER V.

§1. SCHOOL HOURS.   §2. SCHOOL-HOUSE.   §3. STATUTES.

§1 IT will not perhaps be out of place to say a few words about the school hours and school subjects of our forefathers. In a book* published in 1612 we find it stated that the school-time should begin at six o'clock, and the first hour be employed in making Latin exercises, and preparation of class-work should be carried on until nine: then, after a quarter of an hour's recreation†, the scholars should continue until eleven; then two hours' interval; then school again till three or half-past; then a quarter's relaxation, and so work till half-past five. The School was to end with reading a part of a chapter, two staves of a Psalm, and prayers by the Master. So it is coolly recommended that youth and children (some of only seven years of age) should be engaged in Latin for nine hours every day. This was still the custom at Heath School in last century. The Statutes of 1730 say " The Master, Usher, and scholars shall constantly repair to School, and the Schoolmaster and Usher shall begin to teach at six o'clock in the morning, and there continue till five at night, saving betwixt eleven o'clock and one, from the 10th of March to the 10th of October, and from thence to the 10th of March again, from eight o'clock till four, saving betwixt eleven o'clock and one." According to some Statutes in Brearcliffe boys were under *the Usher* until they were perfect in the Grammar, both Accidence and

---

* Brinsley's Book, quoted on p. 3.
† Called at some schools *bever* time *i. e.*, drinking time, from the old French *bevere*, Latin *bibere*.

Syntax, and could "apply* their lectures" in simple books, one of which, Corderius' Colloquies, is especially mentioned. Under *the Master* they had to speak Latin; and the authors they had to read more or less were Tully, Terence, Ovid, Virgil, Cæsar. The Greek Testament is also mentioned, and Hesiod or Homer together with Hebrew Grammar. Latin Themes, and Greek and Latin verses had to be practiced, and the study of Logic was begun. No Mathematics, no English Literature, no Drawing, no Drill, and no ologies of any kind! What barbarians our forefathers must have been! yet some of them had a reputation as learned men.

§2. We have no description of the School and School-house, but in 1727 a return made to the Archbishop of York says "There is a house of three rooms on a floor joining to the School, and a Garden." In 1738 Wright describes it as "a stately Grammar School, whose building is fair, fine, and large, all of free stone, with a good school-house with handsome and convenient apartments for the Head-Master and his family to dwell in." He also says "Over the school-house door are [some] verses, cut in a fair stone, plain and legible." These I have already quoted.

§3. In 1729 the Archbishop's Secretary speaks of the necessity of "drawing up a full body of Statutes for the future Government of the School : 'tis expressly contrary to the interest of the original Charter that such a body of Statutes has not been hitherto framed." But Brearcliffe gives us what he calls "Statutes or Orders to be observed in the Free Grammar School of Queen Elizabeth." These however were rather for the direction of the Masters and Scholars, and were possibly drawn up by Dr. Favour. As they contain many curious illustrations of the manners of the times, I quote them fully in Chap. IX.

---

* *i. e.*, apply or devote themselves to their readings, as we should say.

CHAPTER VI.

MR. Byrron's death in April 1629, left the School for a time in the hands of the Usher. A Mr. Francis Cockman was appointed his successor. A curious letter from Henry Hoile (of Hoyle-house?) to R. Sunderland, dated June 3rd, 1629, says:—"Sᴿ, I have sent this bearer Mr. Cokmā home [i. e. whom] I latlye recommended for yoᴿ scholemaster, he is willing and redy to atend yᵉ divine dispensation: and to abide any faire tryall for yoᴿ aprobation and your satisfaction........." As soon as he got settled in his house, he felt the need of a partner, and on Aug. 24th, 1630, he finds a place in the Parish Registers as married to Grace Ward, and the unusual words, "per Li'am" i. e., by Licence, are put beside their names. Between that date and 1643 the baptisms of six of his children are recorded in that same book, but in 1645 Jan. 28th (i. e. at the end of the year) the burial of Francis the son of Francis Cockman of Southowram occurs. Whether this was the son of our Francis, I do not know, but he was a well-known youth, for Brearcliffe, speaking of the plague, says, "27th January 1645 yong franc. Cockman low brer* buryed." John and Thomas are the only sons of Francis mentioned among the baptisms. There is nothing more to guide us to his death or resignation. He must however have been a good Master, for John Lake (afterwards Vicar of Leeds and a celebrated Bishop) was a

---

* i. e., Low Brear in Southowram as opposed to Upper Brear.

Vicar in 1712, was probably not elected, as in 1727 he writes
to R. Sterne, who had asked him to take the oath before
" Mr. Gream who is the surviving Trustee " :—" I have no
account from my Lord Archbishop of me being appointed
a Governor of the Free School.........Considering my bad
circumstances of health, I cannot think myself capable of
executing the Trust and therefore desire to be excused from
having any share in it ". However, in 1726 and for some
years previous, Henry Gream, one of the four, was the only
surviving Governor. There must have been great neglect;
there was no body left qualified to receive rents, or to
choose new Governors. The then Archbishop (Dr. Lancelot
Blackburn), when he came to enquire into the matter, doubted
whether it was in his power to elect new Governors, as the
Charter seemed to require the consent of two to his proceedings. By his advice a petition was presented to the
King (George I) for a renewal of the Charter. His Majesty
referred it on July 1st, 1726, to his Attorney and Solicitor
General for their opinion, but through pressure of public
business it was not until June 2nd, 1727 (the day before the
King started for Hanover, never more to return) that they
made their report. To save the Corporation, they recommended
a liberal interpretation of the old Charter, which said :—
" He shall be chosen Governor whom the Archbishop of York
for the time being *Sede Archiepiscopali plena* or *Sede eadem
vacante* the Dean of the Cathedral Church of York with
consent of two of the Governors aforesaid shall name
shall be taken and reckoned for a Governor ".* They
recommended that, as there was a doubt, the words " with
consent of two of the Governors " should be taken as

* I put the words as I find them. I have endeavoured to use as much as
possible the language of " the Sterne Correspondence " in this Chapter, and that
must be my excuse for many awkward expressions.

applicable only to the Dean and not to the Archbishop. So narrowly did the Charter escape; and the scholars might defend their own disregard of stops by the benefit that once accrued to their school by it.

Richard Sterne was the chief man in this business. A copy of the correspendence between him and the Archbishop's Secretary (Thomas Haytor) and the London Legal Agent is still in existence, and shews what difficulties there were in the way before the question was finally settled. In consequence of the opinion given, Mr. Sterne* chooses ten other Gentlemen "above 24 years of age, men of worth, and of the Established Church, and entire friends of the Government", as he reports to the Archbishop. This, we must remember, was the time when men feared the Jacobites and the encroachments of Popery. The Archbishop accepts the nominees, confirms the election (Oct. 23rd, 1727), and recommends them to apply to Mr. Gream and take before him the oath of qualification. · Eight of them did so, but the Vicar refused to act, being dissatisfied with the other Trustees who were not willing "to act under his directions;

---

* The following extracts from two Letters now at Shibden Hall and kindly communicated by John Lister Esq. will confirm my statements.
"Mr. Stern and Mr. Burttons Quarrel now I suppose is not a Lawsuit but an affront upon Mr. Sterne by denying him the Sacrament. The names of the ffeoffees as far as I can learn are Mr. Burtton Mr. Stern Mr. Booth Mr. Taylor Mr. Ramsbothom Mr. Stott Mr. Ramsden of Sydall Hall Mr. Ramsden of Wharlehouse Mr. James and Mr. John Batley Mr. Eleana Farrar Mr. Henery Haigh........I fancy they all voted for Turner however y^t they are nominated by Mr. Sterne is unquestionable". (*Letter dated Dec.* 20, 1727.) "Anything y^{ts} worth enquiring after, Mr. Burtton can give you an account of, as consarning the method of Electing Govern^{rs} for ffree school how far Mr. Burtton and his company proceeded And also what encouragemt Mr. Stern has because as I havo heard there is occasion for laying down some mouey wch makes severall wch otherwise would be Govern^{rs} to decline". (*Dated Dec.* 25, 1727.) I find that on May 16th, 1729, Richard Sterne and Rev. Thomas Burton were elected Governors of Hipperholme School. I wonder if they had become friendly by this time.

and, not being able to have all the power, he would not accept of any share of it". So says His Grace, who also through his Secretary writes that "he would not be surprised at anything he (the Vicar) does when his intentions are disappointed". Two others were afterwards led away by him, and resigned. There were difficulties also about the old Charter and the Deeds belonging to the Trust, which had been in the Vicar's keeping, but the Charter was found to have been sent to Bishopthorpe, and the particulars of the Rental* were afterwards sent by the Vicar to His Grace. It seems also that the Vicar had once been ' solicitous ' about the affair, and money had been collected and £70 lodged in a London Attorney's hand. The new Governors were averse to having anything to do with the old Agent, and would not advance any money out of their own pocket, and the matter was brought to a standstill. His Grace's Secretary informed them that the "petty jealousies and suspicions of some of the Governors" would "make it impossible for him (the Archbishop) to do them any service; and he must lay aside all thoughts of concerning himself any further". This roused Sterne, who was determined to make the work good, if only to spite the Vicar. He persuaded his father-in-law† (Timothy Booth), one of the Governors to join him in advancing sufficient money for the purpose. But money was not easy to find. He had repeated demands from the London Attorney for "money out of pocket". However, the originally named Governors were urged by His Grace to petition the Crown for the Charter, notwithstanding

---

* This amounted to only £39 12s. 0d. per annum.

† R. Sterne married for his first wife, in 1703, Dorothy, relict of Samuel Lister and daughter of Thomas Priestley; and for his second Esther Booth, in September, 1714. The Priestleys were connected by marriage with a family in Mixenden named Booth.

the refusal of three to act; and a confirmation of the Charter was at length obtained; and Sterne was, no doubt, rejoiced to read the words:—"In witness whereof we have caused these our Letters to be made Patents. Witness* Caroline, Queen of Great Britain, France, and Ireland, Guardian of the said Realm, at Westminster, the one and thirtieth day of July†, in the third year of our Reign (*i. e.* 1729). By writ of Privy Seal. Cocks".

We will simply add to this that, Mr. Sterne sent the agent about £100 by 1730, and then owed about £60. As he expected this to be repaid, the school revenues were hampered for some years. He did not live long to enjoy his victory; he died in October 1732, and the Governors were then indebted to his Estate. He probably took very little part in the school affairs, after the appointment of a new Master, as he spent his last days principally at the family estate of Elvington, near York, though he was buried at Halifax. His son Timothy, to whom he bequeathed Woodhouse, seems to have had too great a liking for horses to have cared much for boys.

On March 26th, 1730, there was to be a general meeting of the Governors. The Archbishop had requested through Mr. Sterne that they would furnish him with a particular account of the state of the School and its revenues; what money they had for defraying the expense of procuring

---

* Schoolboys if thoughtful, may be surprised at this : but school-histories do not record this Regency of the Queen. Larger Histories will however tell them that George II went to Hanover on May 17th, 1729, and did not return until Sep. 11th. They may feel interested in knowing that what one Queen gave, another Queen confirmed.

† Wright (p. 26) dates the Charter "July 21, 1729"; Crabtree (p. 175.) "7th July, 1730: The Schools Inquiry Commission Report, "30 July, 1730" A copy of the Statutes made in 1842 gives "the twenty-first day of July" as the date of the Charter, and "One thousand sevenhundred and thirteen" as that of the Statutes, (!) So much for Authorities !

---

the Charter; how the land was leased, and what improvement the Estate was capable of; and he promised that he would then send them a complete body of Statutes*. We hope that they did so. Mr. Wilkinson, Mr. Jackson, and Mr. Sharp offered themselves as Candidates for the Mastership, and it was agreed to send them to His Grace's Chaplain for examination. But probably Mr. Sharp withdrew, as he had just obtained a nomination to Sowerby Bridge Chapel, and Mr. Christopher Jackson was eventually elected Master. In a letter of Dec. 29th 1730, Mr. Sterne writes that he had had a great deal of trouble about the School, but hoped that the Master would answer expectation.

---

* The Statutes were sent, discussed by the Governors, and signed by them, three new Governors having been previously elected in the place of those who refused to act.

CHAPTER VIII.

WHATEVER might have been Mr. Stern's expectation, Mr. Jackson's was not answered, for he resigned some time in, 1731, and the Governors had to elect again. Mr. Jackson's successor was Mr. Edward Topham (B.A., 1729; M.A., 1733.,) who became a fellow of Trinity College Cambridge, and probably looked down on such an humble post as the Mastership of Heath School, for he resigned in 1733. Then came the Rev. John Holdsworth, of St. John's College, Cambridge, who, having graduated B.A. in 1710, and M.A. in 1717, was a man of some experience. Why he should take the post at his age, we cannot tell; but perhaps he had it in his power to attract "foreigners", as the non-foundationers were called; for in 1738 Wright says :—"The School is now in a very flourishing condition under the care and conduct of the Rev. John Holdsworth M.A., the present worthy and learned Master". But his income was increased a few pounds per annum on his appointment at once to the cure of Coley by Dr. Legh, the Vicar of Halifax. In 1740 he was presented to the Lectureship of Halifax, a dignity—for it was then a dignity—which he did not enjoy many years, for in 1744 death deprived him of all his earthly employments.

When the Governors proceeded to elect a new Master, they found themselves in a difficulty again, as they had several times been since the foundation of the School! In the place of the three who refused to act under the new

Charter, W. Walker, James Tetlow (or Tetlay), and John Lodge had been elected. But before 1744 six of the twelve were dead and one had left the parish. The five surviving Governors had nominated four others, who had taken the oath of qualification; but when they came to act, no record was found of their having been appointed within the month prescribed by the Charter. Fearful lest their acts might be disputed, they took Counsel's advice, who satisfied their scruples by recommending them to apply to the Archbishop to "establish the persons so appointed in ,the office of Governors". They did so; and also about the same time they appointed three others. Feeling confident that they were now fit to fill up the vacancy caused by the death of Mr. Holdsworth, they elected Samuel Ogden, of St. John's College, Cambridge, (B.A., 1737, M.A., 1741,) to the Master-ship, who "took his corporal oath" June 11th. Mr. Ogden* had been curate of Coley since the end of 1740, and continued there until 1747, when he succeeded Mr. Alderson (who had been promoted to the Rectory of Burghwallis) in the curacy of Elland. He had been elected Fellow of his College in 1739, but he was not too proud to hold a position of usefulness in conjunction with one of dignity, and he continued Master of the School until 1753. He was one of the most learned Masters of Heath School, yet what was his income as such? It varied between £37 and £30 a year! for the debt incurred by the new Charter was not wiped off yet, and some years brought a less return than others. However he got tired at length of the School, and feeling that he was ill repaid

---

* In Dr. Hallifax's brief Memoir of Ogden, prefixed to his Sermons, he is stated to have been elected Master in 1744 and afterwards appointed to Coley: but in the Parish Registers there is a copy of his Licence to Coley dated Feb. 9, 1740, i. e., 1741. N. S. If this date is correct, he was only in Deacon's Orders, having been ordained in June 1740 at Chester.

even by the Mastership and Curacy combined, which did not give him any position worthy his deserts, he resigned the School in 1753, though he kept the Curacy till the end of 1762. He retired to Cambridge and lived on his Fellowship, and became very popular as a preacher in the University. He does not seem to have resided in the School-house for some years before his resignation, for the Governors had in 1748 given him permission to let it and the lands belonging to the School. "He was an excellent classical* scholar", we are told, "a scientific divine, and a proficient in the oriental languages : as schoolmaster, he left a blessing behind him, in having communicated to some who afterwards became teachers themselves his own exact grammatical mode of institution". This however was not a judgment pronounced by anybody at Halifax.

After his resignation the Usher, Mr. Richard Sutcliffe, who was then curate of Lightcliffe and afterwards became Master of Hipperholme School, (where he had the credit of educating Mr. Knight, subsequently Vicar of Halifax,) taught the whole school for several months until Thomas West, who was elected April 25th and qualified Aug. 22nd, entered on his duties at the beginning of September. He was (probably) of Emmanuel College, Cambridge, and graduated B.A. in 1736; but there is no account in the List of Cambridge

---

* It was the practice of the University to send congratulatory verses to the King on the occasion of any public event. Among the contributors in 1762, on the occasion of the marriage of the King, we find "Samuel Ogden, D.D., Senior Fellow of St. John's". We may also add the name of Joah Bates, of King's College, a Halifax man and son of the parish Clerk. He probably received his early education at the School when Mr. Ogden was Master, having been born in 1740.

We may also add that Dr. Craven, who became Professor of Arabic at Cambridge in 1770, declined a bequest of money which Dr. Ogden had given him in a will made sometime before his death, and begged he would leave him instead his Arabic Books.

Graduates of his having proceeded to a superior Degree.
He seems to have been successively curate of Luddenden and
Ripponden. For some cause or other he gave dissatisfaction
to the Governors: he had "to quit the School-house and
land at Candlemas and Mayday" 1770. The Master had at
this time and long afterwards to pay rent for the house and
land, and perhaps Mr. West was unable, like many other
men of learning, to cultivate land and boys equally well.
This notice to quit, no doubt, offended him, and there was
so much ill-will displayed, that the Governors gave him a
"New Year's gift" of £10 in 1771 on condition that he
"quit the School".

In 1770 we find one Richard Hudson Lecturer of the
Parish Church. Now Mr. Hudson was not a graminivorous
animal, and, though he was a fellow of Queen's College,
Cambridge, would hardly have come to the Parish Church
for the sake of a house and garden: he must have had some
pay besides,—but what has become of that, for there has
been none for many years?—yet it was not enough for his
wants, and therefore he gladly accepted the appointment
of Master of Heath School on Jan. 11th, 1771, although the
income was then only £35 a year. But, having a house
as Lecturer, he does not seem to have had his mind disturbed
by farming operations at Heath, and the house and land
were let to the Usher. The School under his management
flourished. In a few years we find the Governors spending
£14 16s. 0d. "for globes &c." though the wonderful things
contained in the "&c." will never be known. The thirsty
souls on the premises were increased, for we find about £32
expended on boring a well and erecting a pump. Perhaps
in Mr. Hudson's time the birch-tree was planted by the
Master's house, as twigs were in request. But Mr. Hudson
was not satisfied: there was not sufficient attraction at

Heath. The Governors seemed to have tried to please him : for in July, 1773, there is an entry in the Minute-book of this kind :—"The present Master and Usher behaving much to the satisfaction of us the Governors we agree to advance the Master's Salary to £50 per ann : and the Usher's to £30 per annum to commence the 24th June last". At a later period, "in consideration of the great increase of scholars", six pounds were given toward the salary of an additional Usher, "the Masters to provide a person and out of their salaries to pay him such further sum as may be necessary, in proportion to the number of foreigners each Master hath under his care "*. There must therefore have been a good number of Boarders. In 1777 "Subscriptions towards improvements at the School" were received to the amount of £240†. The Governors were now so well off that they presented Mr. Hudson with "3 pair Blankets" at the cost of £2 12s. 6d. ! What the improvements were we must imagine : whether they consisted in erecting the dormitories over the School-room or not, we cannot tell, but certainly £12 1s. 0d. was spent on the School Chimney, and enlarging the Kitchen. But there was a stir ; the golden age seemed coming for Heath : yet Mr. Hudson was not content. He thought he could better himself ; and he was elected, April 25th, 1782, Master of Hipperholme School, in place of the Rev. Richard Sutcliffe, who had died on March 17th. He seems to have entered on his duties after the Midsummer holidays, as the Rev. Matthew Moss, the Usher, "officiated as School Master" for some months, the School having probably but few scholars. On Jan. 15th, 1783, the Rev. Gough Willis Kempson was elected Master on a Salary of £80 per annum. Money was now borrowed by the Governors at five

---

* But the rent of the School-house was at the same time advanced £5 per annum.

† In 1777-8 Bills were paid to the amount of over £300.

per cent. interest, in addition to subscriptions of £126 odd.
There is entered in the Accounts of Mar. 12th "Cash for
Plans and Estimates for erecting a new School-house
£1 1s. 0d.", and June 26th "Cash for rearing Free School
House £1 1s. 0d". So that the present house was probably
erected in 1783, nearly 100 years ago. The Master himself
"laid out several hundred pounds in the improvement of
the School and House and Premises thereto belonging".
But he resigned in 1788, the cause unknown; and the
Governors allowed him the sum of £100 "as a consideration"
for the outlay.

On the death of Mr. Sutcliffe in 1782 the Rev. Robert
Wilkinson became Curate of Lightcliffe, entering on his duties
on July 7th. I have not ascertained whether he was then
a Graduate of a University, or whether* he was connected
with the neighbourhood. In 1787 he subscribes one guinea
to the new set of Bells at the Parish Church and is put
down under Hipperholme. He might have been resident
in the Township or even Assistant Master† at the School.
At any rate he was looked on as a competent man to fill the
vacancy at Heath, and on Feb. 4th, 1789, he was elected
Master on a salary of £75 a year, which in 1797 was raised
to £80. The School gained a celebrity under his tuition,
and many "foreigners" resorted to it. At one time the
number was so great that several boarded at a house at
Moor-bottom, which was pulled down a few years ago. I
once heard an old pupil say that there were a hundred
scholars at the School, but most of them were boarders.
Houses however were wonderfully elastic in those days!

Mr. Wilkinson had probably entered his name on the
books of Trinity Hall, Cambridge, which enabled him after

---

* I have heard it said that he was a Cumberland man.
† I have been told that he was Second Master.

ten years, on satisfying the authorities that he had devoted
himself to the study of Theology, to take the Degree of
B.D., without going through the usual course of residence at
the University. Having thus obtained a Degree in 1790, he
proceeded no higher in Divinity, and devoted himself to the
duties of his Mastership. For many years the School had a
great notoriety in the West Riding; and there was a rivalry
between Heath and Hipperholme, the latter claiming a sup-
eriority in "manners" and the former in "brains". In 1826
notwithstanding the age of the Master there were several
boarders and about 35 free scholars. But for some years
before his death, which took place at the end of 1839, there
were very few scholars; and one of them tells me that all
the time was wasted for the three years he was at the School.
Mr. Hudson had also given up Boarders at Hipperholme.
Both Schools consequently ceased to attract any scholars
from a distance for classical education, and became more
or less local Schools. Mr. Hudson died in 1835 and Mr.
Wilkinson in 1839; the former had been Lecturer at the Parish
Church for 65 years, and the latter Curate of Lightcliffe
for 57 years. It is no wonder then that their names should
have once been as Household Words in the Parish. Mr.
Wilkinson continued in harness till almost the last moment
of his life. He was able to attend a dinner given him in
the Town by some fifty of his old pupils on Dec. 19th, 1839,
and in ten days after he breathed his last. On Dec. 3rd
the Governors, who had for some cause allowed him and
his predecessor to appoint the Usher, had resolved to adhere
to the Statutes for the future and to make the election
themselves. This proceeding, which probably concealed some
dissatisfaction, and the excitement of the Dinner, may have
hastened his end. He was buried on Jan. 7th in Lightcliffe
Churchyard. A tablet was erected to his memory in the

Parish Church over the North entrance. The Latin Inscription on it was written by Dr. Lonsdale, Principal of King's College, London, and afterwards Bishop of Lichfield, who before he went to Eton was a pupil of Heath School. Dr. Lonsdale left his name behind him on a pane of the old windows of the School, which were removed in 1861, and on the old Organ Gallery of the Parish Church.

I have about 150 names of pupils who were under him, which were scribbled in the old Dictionaries that I have mentioned, and a few of those pupils are still alive.

The Statutes fixed a period of 6 weeks after a vacancy of the Mastership, within which a new Master was to be appointed, and in the beginning of February, 1840, the choice of the Governors lighted on Edward Sleap, M.A., of Brasenose College, Oxford. He, however, being a Bachelor and frightened at having to become a house-keeper, immediately resigned on seeing the House. In a few days after, the late Archdeacon Musgrave wrote to the Rev. John Henry Gooch, M.A., who was next best candidate; and he accepted the office, and was elected on Feb. 24th. He had been a scholar of Trinity College, Cambridge, and was at the time one of the Masters at Wakefield Proprietary School, under the Rev. Dr. Butterton. Having commenced his duties there, he 'was unable to enter at once on those of Heath School; but, as there were no scholars at the death of the late Master and the house required much to be done to it, he was allowed to put off residence until July. During the first half-year he entered 34 pupils, and gradually increased the number until he had in 1854 more than 70. Many of his pupils went to the University, and several were successful Candidates for the Milner Scholarship. In 1841 he had been appointed to the New Parochial district of Stainland, but for some time exchanged duties with the Lecturer of the Parish Church, Mr. Gilderdale, who resided at Huddersfield.

He died in July, 1861*, and was succeeded by the Rev. Thomas Cox, M.A., who was formerly scholar of St. John's College, Cambridge. He entered on his duties in October. He found 27 boys in the school, which were increased to 38 by the end of the year. Gradually the School increased to 68, when in 1875 the New Scheme promulgated by the Endowed School Commission came into operation. This has hitherto lessened the numbers, as the Fees were considerably increased and boys had to leave the School at the age of 14, unless they were fit for the higher teaching of the Head Master. Several boys went to the University, among whom were a Senior Classic of 1870 and a successful Candidate for the Milner Scholarship. Mr. Cox has been Lecturer of the Parish Church since August 1871, having been appointed to the post by Archdeacon Musgrave, so that, as he said, some position might be given to the Master of the School.

Prior to Mr. Gooch's time nothing seemed to have been taught but Latin and Greek. He however boldly introduced Mathematics in all their branches. To these Mr. Cox added a systematic study of English Literature and the French Language, and a more extensive acquaintance with Divinity. The New Scheme provides for Drawing, Drill, Science, Chemistry, and other subjects; and it is to be hoped that when it comes fully into operation on the completion of the New Buildings, the School will be found inferior to none in the West Riding.

The History of the School will not be complete without something being said about the efforts of Mr. Cox to raise the position of the School in the eyes of the general public. So little was it regarded that the Local Newspapers would not for several years after his appointment admit a paragraph

---

* Shortly after his death a stained-glass window was erected by former pupils and friends to his memory in the Holdsworth Chapel at the Parish Church. The subject is Christ among the doctors in the temple.

about the proceedings on the day of delivery of the prizes, unless it was paid for as an advertisement; but at last they yielded and even sent reporters. The examination of the boys was conducted at Midsummer and Christmas by the Masters, until 1866, when the Governors were induced to provide a special Examiner for the Summer Examination. They also out of their own pockets provided two valuable prizes for Classics, and Archdeacon Musgrave two of equal value for Divinity. The Rev. J. H. Warneford also gave three prizes for the encouragment of boys under thirteen years of age in Divinity, English Literature, and Arithmetic. These were in addition to those given by the Masters. But from circumstances, which need not be mentioned, these all ceased when the New Scheme was acted on; and prizes are now annually given from the School Funds; though the Governors formerly thought that they were not allowed to provide them from such a source.

Such is the uneventful history of Heath School. There is no record of the honest efforts of the Masters to make their pupils into scholars in the best sense of the word. It is impossible to tell the good which each produced in his own day. But I have no doubt that the experience of most was the same as my own. I have had the most complimentary letters from parents, and the most grateful letters from pupils. Many, whom circumstances in after life have brought into the neighbourhood, have called on me, and some have gone out of their way even 50 miles to spend an hour at the School. Many remarks which I have made have produced an effect which I never thought of at the time that I made them, and no examination could possibly have brought out their advantage; yet they have influenced for ever the lives of those who heard them. But I am also bound to say that I have received from the parents of some the bitterest letters that could ever have been written.

I shall say nothing at present about the Report of "The Schools' Inquiry Commission", besides mentioning the insertion in it of a long letter from Mr. Cox, which was considered very valuable. I have taken the following complimentary extracts from the General Report.

"It will be seen by reference to the Report on Halifax, that the interests of the majority of the scholars are not always sacrificed to those of the few who are going to College. The whole are taught together; all share in the supervision of the Head Master; and the whole teaching resources of the School are available for every boy. Some are far advanced in Classical learning; while the rest are receiving an Education in all respects adapted to their wants, and more liberal in its character than that of a Commercial School."

"At Halifax great attention has been devoted by the Head Master to English Literature; and the result has been most satisfactory. The following passage occurs in the Report of the Rev. H. G. Robinson (the Examiner of the School) ; and my own observation fully bears out his testimony:—'I may refer to the Papers in English Literature, as giving evidence of careful teaching and intelligent study. . . A very considerable number of boys showed a really good knowledge of the subjects.'"—*Vol.* ix. *p.* 120.

"All the ordinary school lessons, the task-work, and written exercises, struck me as being much above the average, both as to the skill with which they had been devised, and the accuracy with which they were performed. . . . There is evidence of great diligence in study. . . . . The discipline of the School is excellent."—*Vol.* xviii. *p.* 103.

" 'The old order changeth', but the old School by no means fades from the memory and affection of whilom scholars ".—*(Extract from a letter of an old pupil.)*

CHAPTER IX.

THE Statutes, by which for the most part the School was governed until 1875, are said to have been drawn up by Dr. Hayter, afterwards Bishop of Norwich. In 1727 the Rev. Thomas Hayter was Secretary to the Archbishop of York, and carried on the correspondence on behalf of His Grace with R. Sterne Esq. J.P., when the Archbishop as Visitor of the School was prayed to nominate a new set of Governors. Mr. Hayter told him in 1729, after the new Charter was obtained, that it was for want of Statutes that the difficulty had arisen at Heath School, as if there had never been any before[1], and that His Grace would send "a complete Body of Statutes" as soon as he was informed of certain particulars which he required. He did so in 1730 or 1731· But in Brearcliffe's MSS. there exist certain "Statutes or Orders to be observed in the Free Grammar School of Queen Elizabeth erected for the Vicarage of Halifax". By whom they were drawn up is not known, but they are so curious that they are worth insertion. The bad spelling, the utter disregard paid to stops, the numerous abbreviations, and a peculiar kind of short-hand, make them often very difficult to interpret or decipher, so that I am not sure always of the words. I think however that I have succeeded in every case but *one*.

---

1 "We the present Governors considering the necessity of statutes to be made without which we do adjudge, and have by experience found the School to be maimed and imperfect in itself......do ordain and decree &c." So say the Statutes, as if they had emanated from the Governors.

1. The schoolmaster must be painful in teaching his scholars, a man fearing God, zealous of the truth, of a godly conversation[2], not partial, diligent to train up his scholars not only in other learning and moral virtue, but also in the principles of Christian religion and farther understanding of the Holy Scriptures.

2. The Usher of the School shall be a man sound in religion, sober in life, able to train up the scholars in learning and good manners, obedient to the School-master in all things concerning his office for his manner of teaching and correcting, and shall take upon him the regiment[3] of the whole School in the absence of the Master, and then supply his office both in teaching and correcting.

3. The scholars must endeavour[4] themselves to serve God, obey their parents and masters, and be of a sober behaviour toward all men, whose particular duties be all following:—

(1). That upon the Lord's day and appointed Holydays they come reverently and in due time unto the Church, take a convenient place, hear attentively the Word of God, lay it up in their memories, abuse not those days in play or other vanities; they meditate of the Word and practice it in their lives, pray and praise God publicly in the congregation and privately in their own habitations.

(2). That they take not God's Name in vain by swearing in their ordinary communication, by forswearing, cursing themselves or others, lying, laughing, and vain sporting, idle and light use of God's titles, works, and Word.

---

2 'Conversation', as in the Bible, always means 'conduct', never 'language', which was 'Communication' as in No. (2).

3. *i. e. regimen*, or *government*, as Bacon calls his Essay XXX. "Of Regiment of Health".

4. This expression 'to endeavour oneself' is very common at this time. "That we may......daily endeavour ourselves to follow" *(Coll : for 2 S. aft. Easter)*; "they will evermore endeavour themselves to observe" *(Order of Confirmation)*; "I will endeavour myself" *(The Ordering of Deacons)*.

(3). That they rise early in the morning, reverence their parents, love and obey both father and mother, and give good example to the whole family.

(4). That they come early to the School without lingering, play, or noise by the way, saluting those they meet, bareheaded.

(5). When the Master or Usher or any stranger entereth into the School, that they salute them, rising up dutifully, and presently sit down again with silence and apply[5] their books.

(6). That they wander not up and down in the School, but rest orderly in their appointed place, labour their morning task and appointed lectures with great diligence, striving rather for high commendations of their Master and strangers than for rebuke and blame.

(7). They must join with the Master and Usher both morning and evening in prayer for remission of sins, acceptation in Christ, direction by the Spirit to illuminate their understanding, enlarge their capacities, certify their judgments, and confirm their memories; and hear some chapters daily out of the Old and New Testament read publicly in the school with all reverence and attention, that they may repeat the principal contents thereof, if they be called forth by the Master; and sing daily some place[6] of David in metre to the praise of God for all his mercies with feeling understanding and spiritual rejoicing, with thanks unto God for the founder of the School, and the good benefactors.

---

5. We should now rather say "apply to their books". In No. (8) we have "apply their lecture". So in an old Book called "*The Schoole of Vertue*" (A.D. 1557). "Thy bokes take out, thy lesson then learne, Humbly thy selfe Behave and governe. Therein takying payne, with all thine industrye, Learnynge to get, thy boke well applye". "Apply your study earnestly". *(Sir H. Sidney, A.D. 1566).*

6. *i. e. passage,* as in the phrase "Common places of a book". One of the books used in Schools in 1612 was "The Psalms in Metre", "because children will learn that book with most readiness and delight through the running of the metre, as it is found by experience". *(Brinsley).*

(8). The scholars under the Usher must learn perfectly the grounds of the Latin tongue according to the Accidence[7] and Grammar, skill to decline 'their nouns, know the declensions, case, genders, and numbers; to join substantive and adjective together accordingly, to conjugate their verbs......[8] all moods and tenses with understanding; to understand the concords and conjunctions of all parts of speech, and apply their lectures in Colo Corderius[9a] and the like authors perfectly to the Grammar rule, which being learned by long practice the most days have one hour given to learn to write and be overseen and instructed by the Usher or some at his appointment, that when they can write a legible hand they may from the Usher be promoted to the Master's teaching.

(9). The scholars under the Master must all speak the Latin tongue; the lowest form learn to translate their lectures into English, and out of the English read them again in Latin; the next form be reading Tully,[9b] Terence, and other classic authors, learn to indite epistles scholarlike, first in English, then in Latin, and learn to make themes with good phrase; the next form beside themes must read poetry, make verses with Ovid and Virgil, join Cæsar's Commentaries, Tully's Orations, and Greek Grammar; and the highest form beside Virgil and Ovid and Terence for

---

7. That part of Grammar which relates to the outward form of words was till recently called " The Accidence ", as opposed to the essence of Language. In the Statutes of St. Olave's School, Southwark, we find " As well in Grammar as in Accidence and other Low Books ".

8. Here is a word which I cannot decipher. It is certainly not "thorow" as " Our Local Portfolio " makes it.

9a i. e. in " Colloquiis Corderii ", a series of dialogues in Latin drawn up for the use of Schools. I have seen mention of an edition as late as 1700 by a Master of Eton School.

9b Tully was the name by which Cicero was generally spoken of in former days.

Latin must read the Greek Testament Greek Horace[10a] Hesiod or Homer, the Hebrew Grammar,[10b] and be entered into Logic, make orations, Greek verses, be able to refer their phrases to the places in their authors.

(10). All the scholars under the Master (if Thursday[11] be a play-day) must on Friday in the morning bring epistles with good invention, orthography, and disposition, the lowest form in English, the two next in Latin; the first form every third Friday in verse, every second Friday in Greek prose.

(11). No scholar or scholars of what degree so ever shall absent himself from School any day, especially the day either now or after to be appointed for exercises[12], without special licence first obtained of the Master, and a true testimonial per the hands of his parents for his absence that day, and for the first and second time of absence he shall be corrected with a rod; if he be absent the third time he shall be expelled the School. [No. (12) is omitted; or else the following are wrongly numbered.]

10a Brearcliffe has here made some mistake: I think it should be "Poets" instead of "Horace". It is singular that even in the Old Statutes of Harrow School, no Greek Poet but Hesiod is mentioned.

10b Never was the Hebrew Language more cultivated than in the 17th century. The celebrated John Milner taught his son Hebrew at an age when others were only beginning Latin.

11. In the Statutes of Sandwich School, A.D. 1580, it was appointed that every Thursday after dinner [which was early then, so that boys came to School after dinner at one o'clock], when a certain specified thing was done, the children were to be dismissed to play. In the Statutes of Merchant Taylors' School, A.D. 1561, the holiday is to be on Tuesday in the afternoon or Thursday. I mention this because an attempt has been made to fix these Statutes of Heath to a time subsequent to 1647, when the second Thursday in every month was by law set apart for recreation. But it was evidently the usual day at an earlier period; for in a book published in 1612 it is recommended that the afternoon holiday should be "either the Thursday *after the usual custom* or according to the best opportunity of the place".

12. The Exercises or Prophesyings were held on the last Wednesday in each month. They consisted of Sermons by one or more preachers, which were generally discussed by the clergy after the laity had retired.

(13). If any scholar shall run or go out of School at any time into the town or fields without leave first obtained of the Master, upon his return he shall be severely punished or taxed by his Master.

(14). If any scholar shall give, buy, sell, or change his books, apparel, or any other thing, or filch or steal any thing out of the School, he shall be severely punished : if he be convinced[13] of any like fault the second time, he shall be expelled the School.

(15). They must ever have books, pen, paper, and ink in readiness, and not rent[14] or lose their books but handsomely carry and recarry them.

(16). If any scholar use railing, wrangling, fighting, giving by-names, or offer any the like abuse to his fellows[15] or any stranger in the ways, he shall be severely punished, and if he continue thus to molest and harm others, he shall be expelled the School.

(17). If any scholar brave out contempt against his Master or the Usher, or give out evil words, or be repugnant and refractory to their commandments and rebelliously withstand their correction, or complain of correction moderately given, or tell abroad who are corrected in the School; if he do not presently humble himself and obey the Master and Usher, he shall be expelled the School.

(18). If any scholar shall go undecently in his apparel, and not carry himself reverently in his gesture, words, and deeds, or use long hair on his head[16] undecently or come with face

---

13. *i. e.* "Convicted" as we should now say. See John viii. 46. "Which of you convinceth me of sin?"

14. "Rent" was formerly used where we now say "Rend".

15. *i. e.* "Companions". "The virgins that be her fellows shall bear her company". Ps. XLV. (*Prayerbook Version*).

16. In "The Book of Demeanor" A.D. 1557 we have :—
"Thy head let that be kembd and trimd, let not thy haire be long,
It is unseemly to the eyes, rebuked by the tongue".

I cannot help inserting an amusing direction at the Grammar School of Lewisham. The boys were not "to wear long curled, frizzled or powdered, or

and hands unwashed, he shall be severely punished, and upon the second admonition, if he do not reform, he shall be expelled the School.

(19). If any scholar upon due proof first had shall find[17] either altogether negligent or uncapable of learning, at the discretion of the Master he shall be returned to his friends to be brought up in some other honest trade and exercise of life.

(20). Finally there shall be two prepositors or monitors appointed weekly or longer at the Master's discretion for order and quietness, both in the Church on the holyday and daily in the School and abroad in the town and highways, to set down the faults committed by the scholars without any partiality, and to present their bills[18] to the Master and Usher when they call for them; if they fail herein, they must be punished for the faults committed by others, and what scholar so ever doth not obey these monitors, he shall be subject to the severe censure of the Master or Usher.

———

Such are the Statutes preserved by Brearcliffe: but as appears from note 1, p. 49, they seem to have unknown in 1730. Even if they had been known, they would not

———

Ruffin-like hair, but shall cut their hair and wear it in such sort and manner that both the beauty of their foreheads may be seen, and that their hair shall not grow longer than above one inch below the lowest tips of their ears". The School was founded in 1647.

17. So in Brearcliffe. It may be an error for " be found ", but yet " find " may be used as a neuter verb, though I do not remember an instance. This regulation often occurs in old Statutes; for instance in those of Harrow School: —" Those who are unapt to learn shall after one year's pains taken with them to small profit be removed from the School". " Trade " is not used as we use it now: it simply means " course of life ", as could be abundantly illustrated. I may mention the " Trade Winds " as meaning " the regular or usual Winds ", and not " Winds suitable for trade ".

18 *i. e.* the records of the faults committed.

have answered the requirements of the Archbishop, for it
was through the neglect of the Governors that the School
had nearly lost its Charter. New Statutes were consequently
required which should define the duties of the Governors.
No doubt a draft copy came from His Grace which they
discussed and altered and returned to Bishopthorpe, and
then they received the "authentic seal" of the Archbishop,
as allowed by him. More than two-thirds of them refer to
the duties of the Governors, which are fully detailed. It is
not necessary to mention any of the regulations referring to
them; but a few particulars may be welcome concerning
the others. The Master was to be well affected to the present
settlement in Church and State, (*i. e.* in 1730), to have been
a student at Oxford or Cambridge for *five** years at least,
and to be well skilled, especially in Grammar and the Latin
and Greek tongues. He was to instruct his scholars in the
grounds of religion, and to take to church such as lived in
or near his house; and every Saturday to examine them
in the Church Catechism. He was to read to them, in Latin,
Phædrus, Nepos, Cæsar, Terence, Livy, Tully, Ovid, Virgil,
and Horace; in Greek, the Greek Testament, Xenophon,
Isocrates, Demosthenes, Hesiod, Homer, and Sophocles. He
was no longer expected to teach Logic, or Hebrew; and
the number of Latin and Greek writers was much enlarged.
He was however still to "inform his youth in good nature
and good manners", to teach them "to reverence their
betters in all places, to be courteous in speech to all men,
in their apparel always cleanly, and in their whole carriage
joining decency with modesty, and good manners with good

---

* I do not understand why *five* years should be fixed on, for the degree of B.A.
was conferred about three years and a half after entrance; unless at the date of
the Statutes further residence was required for the degree of M.A.

learning ". Besides the ordinary Grammar, the Usher was to read to his pupils the Sententiæ pueriles, Cato*, and Æsop's Fables.

The Master could be absent only twenty days a year and the Usher sixteen; they might take those days "at once or separately", but both were not to be absent together. I suppose this must have been in addition to the fixed holidays†.

The School-hours were from 6 a.m. to 5 p.m. between March 10th and October 10th, and from 8 a.m. to 4 p.m. the remainder of the year, with a rest between 11 and 1.

The vacations were to be for 15 days at Easter, 10 at Whitsuntide, and 21 at Christmas.

There were considerable alterations made in these Statutes in 1842. The Greek and Latin Authors were to be such as were approved of by the Governors from time to time. The Usher was to take such part of the Education as should be prescribed by the Master, subject to the sanction and control of the Governors. The Masters were to be at liberty to absent themselves during the Vacations (as if the Governors had supposed that throughout the year one or other was to be present at the School). The attendance was to be from 9 to 12, and from 2 to 5. The number of Free Scholars was limited to 60.

In 1873 new regulations were drawn up by the Endowed Schools' Commissioners, and are now in force.

---

* ' Cato ' was the title of a Book on " Good Manners ": it consisted principally of some couplets in Latin Hexameter verse on various duties of the young. It was a favourite book with schoolmasters in the Middle Ages. Its author, and the time of its production, are quite unknown. Chaucer quotes it. Caxton printed a Translation of it.

† This is especially provided for at some Schools, e. gr. at St. Bees, by the insertion of "except" before the fixed holidays; at others, by stating "at such time as School is kept ", or similar language.

The subjects of instruction fixed by them are, in the Junior Department, English Grammar, Composition, and Literature; Arithmetic; Elements of Algebra and Geometry; History; Geography; Latin; Some modern language other than English; Natural Science; Drawing; Vocal Music: and in the Senior Department, Greek, and Mathematics, in addition.

CHAPTER X.

ALTHOUGH mention has already been made of the Masters so far as they affect the history of the School, it will perhaps not be amiss to collect together all that is known of them, partly for the sake of those who take an interest in the School, and partly that others may be guided in their search for additional information about it. Before Newspapers afforded facilities for advertising, the Governors would have to make enquiry among their friends for a suitable candidate; or some member of a College, hearing of the vacancy, would recommend a young friend to the Governors. Hence we see many local names among the early Masters. The qualification of a Master according to the Charter was, that he should be "a meet man learned and cunning* which "hath been student in one of the Universities of this realm "of England the space of five years at the least and hath "profited in learning". As this part of Yorkshire seems to have preferred Oxford to Cambridge in Elizabeth's reign and that of James, most of the early Masters, (and the contemporary Vicars too,) were Oxford men. It is doubtful whether they had been students at either University for

---

* The substantive "cunning" was a good old English word, meaning "skill". Every body knows the phrase in the Psalms, "Let my right hand forget her cunning"! *i. e.* skill in playing on the harp. By the Statutes of Stockport School the Master is required to "be a discrete man and conning in Gramer and be able of connyng to teche Gramer".

five years; but they must so far have profited by their
residence there, as to be fit to prepare others to become
University students. In fact Learning was then a business,
and no one was fit to practise it, until he had gone through
a certain course in a manner satisfactory to the Authorities
of the Universities. It is singular that nothing is said of
the necessity of the Master being in Holy Orders, as was
generally the case in Grammar Schools; nor can we tell
whether the early Masters were so, as it was not the practice
then to put "Rev." before the names of clergymen. Mr.
Greenwood in 1651 is the first, of whom we can positively
say that he was ordained. In the Registers of the time
Mr.*, *i. e.*, 'Magister' seems put only before Graduates of
the University, whether clerical or lay, and the landed
Gentry; a clergyman being more especially designated by
'clericus' or 'clerk', put after his name. At first, the
Schoolmaster was called 'informator', and his duty was
'to inform', *i. e.*, to form or train his pupils *to* learning or
good manners: afterwards he is called 'ludimagister' or
'schoolmaster', *i. e.*, master or head of the school. It was
the Master's duty to read Authors to† his pupils, and call
on them to repeat to him what he had taught them, as
books were scarce. Hence it was that an Usher was required
to prepare the pupils for profiting by the Master's teaching.
I will now proceed to give some account of the Masters.

---

* "He shall be called Master, which is the title that men give to esquires and
gentlemen, and be reported ever after". *(Harrison, abt. 1577).* "He could not
be reckoned among the gentry, though he was called by the name of Mr. Lomax ".
(Memoirs of Colonel Hutchinson). 'Esquire' was not so common then as now:
its use in 1602 may be seen from a passage in a Comedy of that date, called " The
Return from Parnassus ", in which occurs the line,
        " They purchase lands, and now Esquiers are made ".
    † The Statutes of Sandwich School are very particular in stating what books
each " form shall have read *to* them ".

I. 1600—160.. RICHARD WILKINSON, B.A.

This Master seems to have been elected August 20th, 1600, according to a statement of the Governors before a Commission of Enquiry in a chancery suit in 1627. (*L. P. CLII.*) The letter of his Presentation to the Archbishop is dated Aug. 29th; a copy of it is preserved in the Parish Registers, which I will give for the pupils to try their learning on.

Presentatio Rich: Wilkinson ad officiũ M^ri Inform-atoris Scholæ Vicariat: de Halifax.

Reverendissimo in xpo patri ac dnõ, dnõ Matheo Archiĉpo Eborũ, Angliæ Primati et Metropolitano, v'ri humiles filii Gubernatores possessionũ revenconũ et bonorũ Liberæ Gramũticalis Scholæ dnæ Reginæ Elizabeth in p'ochia et vicariatu de Halyfax in com : Eborũ v'ræque Eborũ dieces : Salutem in dnõ sempiternũ. Ad Scholam Gramũticalẽ p'dictam iam vacant' Richardũ Wilkinson in artib^s baccalauriũ p' nos electũ ad officiũ m'ri inform-atoris eiusdẽ scholæ dominationi v'ræ p'sentam^s humiliter rogantes ut p'dictũ Richardu in magistrũ informatorẽ Scholæ p'dictæ admittatis, ceteraq : oĩa et singula p'ficere et p'implere quæ v'ro in hac p'te incubẽt officio. pastorali velitis cũ favore, dat' apud Bradley in vicariatu p'dict' vicesimo nono die Augusti a^o p'dictæ d'næ n'ræ Elizabeth Dei grũ Angliæ, ffranciæ et hyberniæ Reginæ fidei defensor' Quadragesimo secundo. In cui^s rei testimoniũ Sigillũ n'rm cõmune apposuim^s die et anno supradictis.

I know nothing more of this Master. His name was a very common one. There was a family of this name at Brackenbed, a member of which was Vicar of Halifax, 1438-1480. There was another at Elland, connected with the Saviles. One member of it was great grandmother of

Sir John Savile, and his sister Janet also married a William Wilkinson. Three of the Elland family, Henry, John, and William, were students at Oxford. Henry was afterwards Incumbent of Waddesdon, Bucks., and one of the Assembly of Divines, and John was Principal of Magdalen Hall, and afterwards of Magdalen College. He was appointed Tutor to Henry, Prince of Wales, when he matriculated at Magdalen College. There was another family of the name at Bradford. Euphemia, a daughter of Richard Wilkinson of this family, was married to George son of Robert Waterhouse of Harthill, and seems to have lived at Siddal. Another daughter of this Richard seems to have married William Rookes of Rookes' Hall, Hipperholme : their son Jonas became a Fellow of University College.

I have found the following, but do not know whether any of them refers to our Master :—

1594 Married Sep. 15, Rich: Wilkinson & Grace Whitwham. (P.R.)
1598 ,, July 14, Rich: Wilkinson & Dorothy Wilkinson. (P.R.)
1608 ,, Feb. 7, Richardus Wilkinson et Jana Ramsden.
(Elland Register.)

II. 160.—1629. ROBERT BYRRON*.

His name is also spelled in the Parish Register Byron and Birron, in Brearcliffe Burron, as well as Byrron†. There is also Biron, among the disbursements of money for the School, in L.P. CLI. In L.P. No. LV., there is a copy of an account of sums of money received by him, from which it appears that he was Master in 1603. He there signs himself Byrron.

---

* He may have been of a Halifax family, as there occurs in P.R. under 7 Feb. 1600, the burial of " Thoms : Byron Hal".

† There was a Curate of Sowerby at the end of the century whose name is written Baron, Barron, Berron, Burron, Burron, and Byron in the Waterhouse Charity Accounts.

Married 1604, Oct. 16. { Robt. Byron Informator Scholæ Grã.
{ Grace Deane (P.R.)

Buried 1629, April 28. Robt. Birron Sk. publicæ Scholæ
Gramaticalis secundus a fundatione
magister. (P.R.)

He is said to have given two books to the Parish Church
Library*, viz, "Aretinus Felinus (*i. e.* Martin Bucer) on the
Psalms", and "Thomas Aquinas on the Evangelists".

One Daniel Foxcroft, of Weetwood near Leeds, who was
Mayor of Leeds in 1665 and died 1691, the son of Samuel
Foxcroft and Grace Lister, married "Abigail, daughter of
Mr. Birron†". She might have been a relation of our
Master. A Daniel Foxcroft acted as one of the Attorneys
of the School in connection with the lands given by the
Saviles, was a Churchwarden in 1599, a Subscriber of £3
towards the completion of the School-buildings, and a
Governor in 1607. A Daniel Foxcroft also gave £5 in 1635
towards the Endowment. He is described as "living out
of the Vicarage"; also, "late of Ealand Hall, Gent". One
of the Wades married a Judith Foxcroft, of New Grange,
near Leeds.

III. 1629—164.. FRANCIS COCKMAN.

This Master seems strangely to have escaped the
notice of Watson, although he is three times in the
Parish Registers called 'ludimagister' or 'publicus
ludimagister'. His marriage is thus entered:—

1630 Aug. 24. { Francis Cockman publ. ludimag.
{ Grace Ward per Liäm. Skir.

---

* This Library received a large number of Books from Simon Sterne, the
Father of Richard Sterne. They seem to have been principally presentation copies
made by their authors to Abp. Sterne, his father.

† See The Pedigree of Foxcroft in *Ducatus Leodiensis.*

Six Children are mentioned as baptised between 1631 and 1643, Esther, Anna, Mary, John, Grace, and Thomas. There was a family at Lightcliffe of that name in 1649, for we find a, Mr. Cockman rated to Lightcliffe Chapel, as the occupier of a seat; and it was Mr. Henry Hoile of Lightcliffe, who recommended Francis Cockman to R. Sunderland, a Governor of the School, as a suitable Master. The Registers also tell us of a Francis Cockman of Southowram in 1645; and of one Elizabeth Cockman of Southowram, buried in 1679: also of the burial of the Widow of Richard Cockman of Warley in 1669.

In conjunction with the Governors, H. Ramsden and R. Sunderland, in 1629, he signs a recommendation of one Mr. Crag for the office of Usher; and in 1634 he is thrice mentioned as witness to a document concerning the transfer of property to the Governors. *(L.P. CLV, CLVI.)*

Thomas Cockman, Master of University College (1722-1744) was son of a Clergyman in Kent. I have also met with the marriage of the daughter of a John Cockman, M.D., about 1725 or so.

IV. 16..—1651. —— MARSH, or MARCH.

Watson merely says "Master in 1649, as appears from the book belonging to Mr. Waterhouse's Trustees".

In this book I find the following two entries:—

1649 "Paid to Mr. March Mayster of the ffre skoll".

1650 "To Mr. Marshe M^r of ffreeschoole".

V. 1651*—1666. PAUL GREENWOOD.

The Greenwoods seem to have been as numerous in the Parish of Halifax as they are now. In the early part of

---

* 1651 Dec. 24 "To Mr. Greenewood Mr of the freschoole £1 0s. 0d." This entry in the Waterhouse Charity Books shews that Watson was wrong in giving 1652 as the date of his appointment.

the century a Charles Greenwood, who had been fellow
of University College, was a travelling Tutor to Thomas
Wentworth, afterwards Earl of Strafford, and subsequently
Rector of Thornhill from 1612 to 1644, and his friend and
counsellor concerning his estates. He was also one of the
trustees to whom the estates of the Earl, which had been
lost by his attainture, were conveyed on their restoration
by the King. He was a benefactor to University College.
In 1635 he gave £20 to Heath School, and subsequently
bequeathed money for a School at Heptonstall, by a will dated
July 14th, 1642. There were also two Daniel Greenwoods
of Sowerby, of whom I have already spoken, and others.
But I do not find how our Master was connected with them.
In 1654 he married one Judith Newton, and had several
children, mentioned in P.R. There is a daughter of one
Mr. Paul Greenwood of Methley, mentioned as buried at
Halifax in 1670. But I do not find that our Master was
connected with Methley at all. He is mentioned in 1658
and 1664 as Curate of Illingworth. He resigned the Mastership on being appointed to the Vicarage of Dewsbury, to
which he was instituted May 29th, 1666*. He died Feb. 1st,
1667-8. The only mention I have found of him is that on
Jan. 31st, 1659, he preached a sermon at the funeral of Jonas
Hemingway of Mytholme, an abstract of which in shorthand
is still preserved at Shibden Hall.

VI. 1666—1688. JOHN DOUGHTY.

There are several Doughtys mentioned in connection with
Ovenden; for instance Michael, whose name occurs in Dr.
Favour's first list of subscribers to the School; and John,

---

* Here again Watson is wrong in his date. He appears in the Waterhouse
Charity Books as "maister of yᵉ ffreeschool" under Dec. 30, 1665, though Watson
says he resigned in 1664.

who is mentioned as being of the University of Oxford in 1640. There was also a John Doughty, fellow of Merton College in 1618, which may be the same as the preceding. A John Doughty graduated B.A. at Cambridge in 1663, being of Caius College : but there is nothing to shew whether our Master was an Oxford or Cambridge man. The entries in P.R. which relate to him are :—

Bap. 1668 Feb. 22 ⎫
Buried „ Mar. 7 ⎬ Jana Mᵣⁱ· Jo : Doughty   Skircoat

„ 1669 Oct. 31 Ux : [*i.e.* wife] Mᵣⁱ· Jo : Doughty Skircoat

„ 1688 Oct. 14 Mᵣ· Jones Doughty de Skircote Ludi Magister.

He received his last payment from the Waterhouse Charity on Sep. 5th, 1688.

In 1681 a John Doughty, perhaps a relative, became Master of Repton School.

***

VII. 1688—1728.   THOMAS LISTER, M.B*.

There were several families of Lister in this neighbourhood, but I have not been able to connect him with any. There was a Craven family of the name, some of whom were noted physicians, but our Master does not appear in their pedigree.

Thomas Lister graduated M.B. at Cambridge in 1688, being of Jesus College. Among the subscribers to new Almshouses for the Waterhouse Charity in 1724 are

"Timothy Booth   1s. 0d.
"Mr. Lister of freeschool 10s. 0d..

I have said so much about him in the History, and in the account of Laurence Sterne, that I have nothing more to say here. The only entry in P.R. is, "Buried 1728, April 25, Mr. Thos. Lister, Skircoat, Schoolmaster".

***

* The qualifications of the Master in Bristol School were "Master of Arts, a Bachelor of Laws or *Physic*, of two years standing".

A Thomas Lister, B.A., whom Wright calls M.A., was Curate of Southowram from 1718 to 1730, perhaps a relation. His successor's Licence at any rate bears date August 1730. (P.R.) He may have been a son of the Master. The signatures of the two in the Waterhouse Charity Accounts are very much alike; and the younger one signs for the elder in 1727.

‗ Since the above was in type, I have seen a memorandum book of Mr. James Lister, of Shibden Hall, for 1703, in which he says "Paid to Coz. Lister of free school . . . ten shillings". I have also seen the Ledger of the principal Apothecary of Halifax, in which there are numerous accounts due from Thomas Lister of free school, and among them " Harry Scolfeild's bill ", he being probably a boarder.

VIII*. 1730—1731. CHRISTOPHER JACKSON, B.A.

There were many Jacksons who held livings at Doncaster and the neighbourhood, Adel, Penistone, and Sowerby, just before his time. Two were named Christopher, one at Doncaster and one at Sowerby. Perhaps he was connected with their family.

He soon resigned his post: and nothing more is found about him. Even his signature does not occur in the Waterhouse Charity Books.

IX. 1731—1733. EDWARD TOPHAM, B.A.

Topham seems to have been a common clerical name in Yorkshire. Seven of that name held livings in Craven within 100 years. The most celebrated one of that name was Francis Topham, LL.D., 1739, Dean of the Arches in York in the middle of the eighteenth century†. There was a monument in old Doncaster Church to an Edward Topham, who was born about 1752, and had been educated at Trinity College, Cambridge.

* There was no Master from April 1728 to some time in 1730.
† He was satirised by Laurence Sterne. See *Fitzgerald's Life of Sterne.*

68

Our Master graduated B.A. at Cambridge in 1729, being of Trinity College, of which he afterwards became a Fellow. Wright gives Matthew as the name of our Master. It is singular that there was a Matthew Topham of St. John's, who graduated B.A. in 1727, and was consequently at St. John's when Wright was. Perhaps he was a relation and assisted Edward.

Edward Topham, according to Watson, published a sermon preached in Selby Church, of which I know nothing.

X. 1733—1744. JOHN HOLDSWORTH, M.A.

This Master may have been a relation of Thomas Holdsworth, who had the Cure of Southowram from 1730 to 1746.

He was licenced Curate of Coley in Nov., 1733, but I do not know whether that was before or after his appointment to the Mastership. He vacated that Cure on being appointed Lecturer of the Parish Church in July 1740, apparently on the resignation of the Rev. Francis Parratt*, who had been Lecturer for 50 years. He was married, for shortly after his death there appears in the Governors' accounts an entry of a sum of money paid to " Widdow Holdsworth ".

His burial is thus entered in P.R.:—

" 1744, Apr. 27., The Rev. John Holdsworth M.A. Lecturer and Master of the Free School of Halifax ".

XI. 1744—1753. SAMUEL OGDEN, M.A.

" June 11. Mr. Samuel Ogden was on the . . . day of this instant duly nominated. The said (S. O.) has took his Corporall Oath." *(Governors' Minute Book.)*

* Spelled Parrott, Parrot, Perrott, Parratt, Parrat. Mr. Holdsworth's Licence is dated July 8th, 1740, but Mr. Parratt did not die till December 23rd, 1741. He spells the name himself *Parratt* in signing a receipt.

REV. SAMUEL OGDEN, D.D.

From a Chalk Drawing in the Master's Lodge, St. John's College, Cambridge, by the kind permission of the REV. W. H. BATESON, D.D.

PHOTOGRAPHED BY T. ILLINGWORTH, HALIFAX.

He was the most celebrated of all who became Masters of the School, and we have a good deal of information about him. He was born at Manchester, July 28th, 1716, the son of Thomas Ogden a dyer, and the grandson of an old Puritan Divine. He was educated at the Grammar School of Manchester, Henry Brooke of Oriel College being then Master. He went up to Cambridge in 1733 as subsizer* of King's College, but in 1736 migrated to St. John's, where he became Scholar, and in March 1739 Fellow. He graduated B.A. 1737, M.A. 1741, B.D. 1748, D.D. 1753. He was appointed Curate of Coley when only in Deacon's Orders, in Feb. 1740-1†, and Curate of Elland in June 1747. He was ordained Deacon by the Bishop of Chester in June 1740, and Priest by the Bishop of Lincoln in November 1741. He resigned his Mastership in March 1753, and then went to reside on his Fellowship at St. John's, but he continued to hold the Curacy of Elland until 1762. His successor was George Burnet, whose Licence is dated Jan. 19th, 1762. Watson puts Burnet's appointment in Nov. 1747, but he probably became Ogden's deputy then. In 1753 the Duke of Newcastle, Chancellor of the University, visited Cambridge, and was present at the Disputation which Mr. Ogden conducted for his Degree of D.D. His Grace was so pleased with his performance, that he afterwards presented him to the Vicarage of Damerham in Wiltshire, an appointment which he could hold with his Fellowship. In 1758 he published two sermons which he preached before the

---

* A subsizer would be one of the lowest of the sizers, or waiters on the fellows. This institution helped to raise many men of greater wits than means to high positions in the University.

† How little we can depend on printed books! In a Memoir prefixed to his sermons by Dr. Hallifax he is spoken of as being elected Master in 1744, and *then* appointed to Coley, but his Licence is dated 1740, according to the copy in P.R. Thoresby also says that he was *afterwards* appointed to Coley.

University, and prefixed to them "a handsome dedication" to His Grace. In 1764 he was appointed to the Woodwardian Professorship of Geology: it shews the sad state of things at that time, that he had to pay 100 guineas* for his appointment. In 1765 and 1776 he was an unsuccessful Candidate for the Mastership of the College. In 1766 he exchanged the living of Damerham, which was so far from his beloved Cambridge, for the Rectory of Stansfield in Suffolk; and in the same year was presented by his College to the Rectory of Lawford in Essex. He had never been an idle man: for some time, after he went to reside on his Fellowship, he had the charge of St. Sepulchre's Church in Cambridge, where he "was constantly attended by a numerous audience, consisting principally of the younger members of the University". It is a pity that Halifax could not retain him, but Schoolmasters do not find much favour anywhere; and it is a wonder that he stayed here so long as he did, for his income, varying with the proceeds of the School estates, was in 1744 only £35, in 1745 £37, in 1738 £31 10s., and 1748 £30, though in the latter year the Governors gave him "liberty to let the School-house and lands", he probably having a house at Elland to reside in. He had a paralytic stroke in 1777 and died March 22nd, 1778; he was buried in St. Sepulchre's Church.

I will add to this a brief description of him, derived from Whitaker's edition of Thoresby's Ducatus Leodiensis. He was stout, athletic, sallow, stern, and had vivid black eyes. The tone of his voice was deep and solemn. His manner in preaching was impressive; his sentences were concise and pointed; his style was of the purest taste. "He was one of those gifted orators who equally attract the learned and the illiterate; who are heard with equal

---

* So says Nichols in his *Literary Anecdotes*.

admiration and delight in the pulpit of a University or by
a congregation of peasants* ". Add to this what I have
said in Chap. VIII. I have also found in the writings of a
contemporary the following statements, worth preserving.
After speaking of him as "a very eccentric character ", he
says :—"He was a man of good property; and, although in
many instances very penurious, yet he was remarkably fond
of good living, and had upon one occasion characterised the
goose as a silly bird—too much for one, and not enough for
two. He would dine out whenever he had an opportunity, but
pleaded his age and infirmities for asking no one in return ".

"He was always unsuccessful in his applications for preferment. It was only his reputed wealth that made him
a *produceable* man, for he was singularly uncouth in his
manner, and spoke his mind very freely upon all occasions ".
"From the singularity of Dr. Ogden's manner, as well of
his matter, he was very popular in the pulpit: he preached
at the Round Church [*i. e.*, St. Sepulchre's], which was
always crowded. His successor in the parish was Dr. Hallifax,
who affected his tone and manner of delivery, but did not
succeed in attracting so numerous a congregation ".

Dr. Hallifax published a volume of Dr. Ogden's sermons,
which he had prepared for the press before his death.
They are 52 in number, and so brief, that each would take
about ten minutes to read aloud: in fact he had adopted
the unusual method of reducing them to the smallest possible
compass, so that the passages of Scripture which are quoted
seem out of all proportion to the rest of the sermon. They
were popular enough to be reprinted: indeed the copy which
I possess is the Fourth Edition. In the Memoir prefixed
to them Dr. Hallifax says :—"In common life there was
a real or apparent rusticity attending his address, which

* "The celebrated preacher, Dr. Ogden". *Nichols' Illustrations.*

disgusted those who were strangers to his character. But this prejudice soon wore off, as the intimacy with him increased : and notwithstanding the sternness and even ferocity he would sometimes throw into his countenance, he was in truth one of the most humane and tender-hearted men I have known ".

I will conclude this account with a *bon mot* attributed to him. One day he was at a dinner given by Lord Hardwick to the Authorities of the University, when a butler drew a bottle of pale brandy by mistake for champagne. The Doctor emptied his glass. His Lordship at once expressed his surprise that he had not noticed the mistake. "I did not remark it to you, my Lord ", said he, "because I felt it my duty to take whatever you thought proper to offer, if not with pleasure, at least in silence ".

" He published two sermons, preached before the University in 1758; one from 1 Thess. v. 13, on May 29th, being the anniversary of the Restoration of King Charles II; the other from Deut. iv. 6, on June 22nd, being the anniversary of His Majesty King George II ". "He also published some sermons on the efficacy of Prayer and Intercession ".

" Soon after the death of his father in 1766, he wrote a Latin Epitaph to his memory, and caused it to be fixed at his own expense on a marble tablet in the Collegiate Church in Manchester ".

XII. 1753—1771. THOMAS WEST, B.A.

He was elected in April 1753, and sworn in on August 22nd; he entered on his duties in September. He was in Orders, when elected. The only Graduate of the name, that I can find, was of Emmanuel College, Cambridge, B.A. 1736.

A Thomas West was Curate of Luddenden from 1761 to 1769, and of Ripponden from 1770 to 1795. The Ripponden Register says "The Rev. Mr. T. West A.B. entered to the

curacy of Ripponden 15 July 1770 ". On his gravestone he is mentioned as having died Nov. 1st, 1795, in the 82nd year of his age. His wife Mary died March 27th, 1784, in the 74th year of her age.

Among the marriages in 1747, in P.R., we find "July 14, Tho: West, Clerk, and Mary Allenson Hal. Spr.", so that he was probably resident in this neighbourhood before his appointment to Heath School.   .

XIII. 1771—1782.   RICHARD HUDSON, M.A.

He graduated B.A. at Cambridge in 1768, being of Queen's College. He was the Eighth Wrangler of his year, and became Fellow of his College. He proceeded M.A. in 1771. In 1770 we find him Lecturer of the Parish Church; and on June 11th, 1771, he was elected Master of the School, an office which he held until his election to Hipperholme School, April 25th, 1782. He removed there in the following June. He is mentioned in 1787 under Halifax as subscribing £5 5s. 0d. to the New Bells at the Parish Church. He seems to have been connected with Hipperholme by birth. In 1739 one Rev. Thomas Hudson is described as "late of Hipperholme" in a tablet to the memory of a child buried at Coley. He became Master of Bingley School and died in 1756. He had another son Thomas who became Fellow of Christ's College, and was, if I am not mistaken, Vicar of Idle, and died Master of Bingley School, in 1785. He had also a daughter Martha, who was the second wife of the Rev. Richard Hartley, Vicar of Bingley. Their son, who was also named Richard, was Master of the School and Vicar of Bingley, and married as his second wife Martha, the daughter of our Master. But there are earlier notices of the Hudsons both at Bingley and Hipperholme. Thomas Hudson of Bingley brings before the Pious Uses Commission in 1619 notice of the will of Michael Broadley. Matthew

Broadley the founder of the School at Hipperholme, had
lands there, and Mr. Sunderland afterwards added to the
endowment out of lands at Bingley. A Richard Hudson had
a seat in Lightcliffe Church in 1634; and a Martha Hudson's
name also occurs in a List of Missionary Subscriptions in
1653, preserved by Brearcliffe. Hence we may infer that
when Richard Hudson left Heath for Hipperholme, he went
there for the sake of old associations, many generations of
his family having lived in that Township. He died March
28th, 1835, and was buried at Coley. There is a Tablet to
his memory in the Church, on which it is recorded that
he was "Master of Hipperholme 53 years, 65 yrs Lecturer
of Halifax, Incumbent of Bolderstone* nʳ Sheffield, and Vicar
of Cockerham nʳ· Lancaster. Integer Vitæ".

In P.R. 1661 Oct. 16. buried, "Rich: Rich: Hudson Hipp".

   ,,   1727 June 11. married "Abraham Speight Clothʳ &
               Drusillah Hudson of Hipperholme ".

In 1731, Thomas Hudson had a lease (£9 per ann:)
from the Waterhouse Charity, as appears in the Charity's
Accounts.

In 1734, Thomas Hudson is a Trustee under Grace
Ramsden's will by which lands in Bingley were given for
a School in Elland.

1746. Dec. 5, married at Lightcliffe, "Mr. Josh. Garthside
               and Mrs. Unice Hudson ".

1790. Jan. 21, buried at Coley, "Elizʰ Wife of Richᵈ Hudson,
               Clerk, Hip ".

XIV. 1783—1788. GOUGH WILLIS KEMPSON, M.A.

He was of Christ Church, Oxford, B.A., 1773; M.A., 1779.

He was in Orders: he is styled Rev. as a subscriber to
the Parish Church Bells of £1 1s. 0d. in 1787. He was

---

* Called also Bolsterstone, and Bolterstone, near Wortley.

"nominated and elected" Jan. 15th, 1783, Mr. Moss* having carried on the School from June to December 1782. He was evidently of an antiquarian family, as both Gough and Willis were celebrated antiquarians. He resigned his Mastership Dec. 11th, 1788.

XV. 1789—1839. ROBERT WILKINSON†.

He was 'nominated' Dec. 18th, 1788, and 'elected' Feb. 4th, 1789, according to the Governors' Book. In 1790 he was appointed Vicar of Darton near Barnsley on the death of Mr. Fisher in August, by Col. Beaumont. His salary was at first £75, afterwards increased to £80. In 1826, the Charity Commission recommended an increase to his salary, the Governors having been saving up money for other purposes; they say " It appears to us, regard being had to the amount of the revenues and to the services of the present Master (to whose stipend no addition appears to have been made for upwards of thirty years) that he has a fair claim to a very considerable increase of salary, and that however commendable it may be to provide for the future prosperity, in point of revenue, of the charity, that object has in this instance obtained too exclusive a degree of attention, at the expense of him who is to be considered principally interested in the trust property, as tenant for life ". *(Crabtree, p. 177)*. In March 1827 the Governors

---

* I am told that the Rev. Anthony Moss, who was afterwards Curate of Illingworth, was one of the Masters of the School: but the Governors speak of a Rev. Matthew Moss, whose widow is mentioned in 1799 in their Books.

† He was in Orders before 1777, for he signs a marriage certificate in P.R. on Jan. 5th, 1777, as "Assistant Curate of Lightcliffe". He became Curate of Lightcliffe in 1782, entering on the Curacy on July 7th. On July 15th, 1782, he married Sarah Robinson of Hipperholme at the Parish Church. He is said to have been a native of Cumberland, which county he visited often ; but in Coley Register there occurs a baptism of a daughter of Robt. Wilkinson of Hipperholme in 1763, and a burial of Robt. Wilkinson of Shelfe in 1789.

resolved that "the Mr. receive the whole Income of the Charity, deducting the actual expenses, and also receive the interest on sum reserved for contingencies . . . and exercise his discretion in the choice and payment of an Usher ".

There is an account of the dinner given him just before his death in the Halifax Guardian of Dec. 21st, 1839.

The Tablet erected to his memory in the Parish Church is as follows :—

M. S.

Roberti Wilkinson   S. T. B.

Scholae Pvblicae in agro Skircotiano ,

Annos plvs qvam L.

Praefecti Optvmi.

Vixit ann. LXXXVI.   Decessit A. S. MDCCCXXXIX.

   Et Sarae vxoris eivs praestantissimae.

Vixit ann. LXXIII.   Decessit A. S. MDCCCXXXIII.

Erat ille si qvis alivs

In pveris institvendis

Strenvvs Solers Sanctvs.

Haec vero in domestica discipvlorvm cvra

Cvstos vnice fidelis

Patrona benignissima

Et tantvm non mater.

Ossibvs amborvm in eodem sepvlcro

Provt mvtvvm amorem decebat

Alibi conditis

Hoc monvmentvm pietatis ergo

Grati alvmni

P. C.

All his old pupils speak highly of Mrs. Wilkinson, who is described in the epitaph as "tantum non mater", *i. e.*, "all but a mother". He had a large family. I have counted eight in the Lightcliffe Register, sons and daughters, but they died young except three (?) daughters, two of whom were married.

REV. JOHN HENRY GOOCH, M.A.

From a Photograph, by the kind permission of MRS. SMITH *and* MISS GOOCH.

PHOTOGRAPHED BY T. ILLINGWORTH, HALIFAX.

XVI*.   1840—1861.   JOHN HENRY GOOCH, M.A.

Mr. Gooch was a native of Suffolk, and educated by his father, until he went up to Trinity College, Cambridge, where he gained several Prizes and a Scholarship. He graduated B.A. in 1834, when he was 14th Wrangler, and in the 3rd class of the Classical Tripos. He became M.A. 1837. From 1838 to 1840 he was Assistant Master at Wakefield Proprietary School, under the Rev. G. A. Butterton, B.D. He was for two years Incumbent of Alverthorpe, near Wakefield. By marrying the daughter of F. Maude, Esq., of Alverthorpe, he brought back into the parish of Halifax a descendant from the old family of the Maudes who lived in Stainland more than 300 years ago, a member of which family was Vicar of Wakefield in Dr. Favour's time, and figures in his subscription List.

Mr. Gooch published a Sermon on the death of Mr. Atkinson, Curate of Elland; an Address to "the Halifax Church School Teachers' Association" in 1854; and a book on the Church Catechism for Schools, which reached a second edition in 1860.

He died July 22nd, 1861, leaving behind him a widow, but no children.

XVII.   1861.   THOMAS COX, M.A.

Mr. Cox received his education at Birmingham Grammar School under the Rev. Dr. Jeune (Late Bishop of Peterborough) and the Rev. Mr. Lee (Late Bishop of Manchester). He proceeded to St. John's College, Cambridge, where he gained several Prizes, and became a Foundation Scholar of the College and Sub-sacrist. He took his degree of B.A. in 1845 and M.A. 1848. He was 35th Sen. Opt., and 5th in

---

* Mr. Sleap's name is omitted from the list, as, though elected, he never took the Official Oath.

the First Class of the Classical Tripos. He was one of the
Masters at the Preston Grammar School from 1850 to 1857,
and Principal of Avenham House School from 1858 to 1861.
He was elected Master of Heath School, August 28th, 1861,
out of 45 Candidates, and qualified September 18th.

In July 1871 he was nominated by the Ven. Archdeacon
Musgrave, Vicar of Halifax, to the office of Afternoon
Lecturer at the Parish Church, an appointment by which
he also acts as Chaplain to Waterhouse's Charity.

He has published "Two Lectures on the state of Education
in the Sixteenth Century", 1869 : and "Six Sermons delivered
at the Parish Church, Halifax", 1878.

He has also delivered in Halifax Lectures on "Education
in the Sixteenth Century", "Universities and Degrees",
"The Tale of Troy Divine, illustrated by readings from
Homer", "The Patron Saints of England, Scotland, and
Ireland", "The Dark Ages", "Influence of the Church on
the State prior to the Reformation", "The Amenities of
Etymology", "Words", "The History of the Formation of
the Book of Common Prayer", "The Irruption of the
Barbarians into Europe", and some others. He also wrote
the Address presented to the late Archdeacon Musgrave on
completing his eightieth year, the inscription on the Verger's
Mace presented to the Church by the Archdeacon's sons,
the Libretto of Dr. Roberts' "Jonah", and Verses on the
occasion of the public thanksgiving for the recovery of the
Prince of Wales in 1872.

The Election of the Master had to be confirmed by the
Archbishop of York, until the new Scheme of the Endowed
Schools Commission. I do not know whether the Master-elect
had to appear in person before His Grace. The only trace
of a "Presentation", which I have found since that of the

First Master, is in an entry in the Governors' Books under 1753 :—"Drawing y^e Presentation 3.. 6.", a lawyer's fee, probably. As I have already given the first, I will now give the last "Presentation".

To the Most Reverend Father in God Charles Thomas by Divine Providence Lord Archbishop of York primate of England and Metropolitan or to any person or persons having sufficient authority in this behalf.

We the Governors of the Free Grammar School of Queen Elizabeth in the Parish and Vicarage of Halifax in the County of York the true and undoubted Patrons of the Mastership of the said Grammar School send Greeting.

We present to your Grace our well beloved in Christ The Reverend Thomas Cox, Clerk, Master of Arts, (who hath been duly nominated and elected by us Master of the said Grammar School in the room of the Reverend John Henry Gooch Clerk, Master of Arts deceased the last Master thereof) for your Grace's approval as Master of the said School. And we do humbly pray that you would be graciously pleased to approve of such our nomination and election.

In witness whereof we have hereunto affixed our Common Seal this twenty eighth day of August in the year of our Lord one thousand eight hundred and sixty one.

CHAPTER XI.

LISTS OF MASTERS, USHERS, AND SPECIAL EXAMINERS.

1. MASTERS.

1600—16..	Richard Wilkinson, B.A.		
16..—1629	Robert Byrron		Died, April, 1629
1629—164.	Francis Cockman		
	—— March, *or* Marshe*		
1651—1666	Paul Greenwood	Curate of Illingworth	Resigned
1666—1688	John Doughty, M.A.		Died, Oct , 1688
1688—1728	Thomas Lister, M.B.		Died, Apr., 1728
1728—1730	(No Master)		
1730—1731	Christopher Jackson, B.A.		Resigned
1731—1733	Edward Topham, B.A.		Resigned
1733—1744	John Holdsworth, M.A.	{ Curate of Coley { Lecturer of Halifax	Died, Apr., 1744
1744—1753	Samuel Ogden, M.A.	{ Curate of Coley { Curate of Elland	Resigned
1753—1771	Thomas West, M.A.	{ Curate of Luddenden { Curate of Ripponden	Resigned
1771—1782	Richard Hudson, M.A.	Lecturer of Halifax	Resigned
1783—1788	Gough Willis Kempson, M.A.		Resigned
1789—1839	Robert Wilkinson	{ Curate of Lightcliffe { and Vicar of Darton	Died, Dec., 1839
1840—1861	John Henry Gooch, M.A.	Curate of Stainland	Died, July, 1861
1861	Thomas Cox, M.A.	Lecturer of Halifax	

* Mentioned in 1649 & 1650.

As many persons feel an interest in Autographs, I lay before them a page for their gratification. All but Mr. Gooch's and Mr. Cox's are to be found in the Account Books of the Waterhouse Charity, appended to receipts for a sum of money bequeathed by Nathaniel Waterhouse to the School. R. Sterne and R. Taylor were the Governors appointed in 1730 to receive the sums payable to the estate. Since Mr. Wilkinson's time the bequest has been paid directly to the Governors.

Hen Greame

Ri: Sterne.   Rich: Gaylor

———————

Thomas Lister. Edward Topham

John Holdsworth

Sam: Ogden.   Tho: West

Richard Hudson.

R Wilkinson   J Henry Gooch

Thomas Cox

Years in which their names are mentioned.	2. USHERS*.
160.	—— Hubert (L.P.)
1629	—— Crag, a Graduate of Cambridge. (B.)
1632	Robert Bolton, buried May 11th, 1632. (P.R.)
1671	(?) Thomas Preston, described in P.R. as Ludimagister.
1727	(?) Abraham Milner†.
1744 Jan.11	Richard Sutcliffe, Curate of Lightcliffe in 1752; Master of Hipperholme School before 1771; died 1782.
1757	—— Fish.
1759	—— Bland.
1763	George Hutchinson, resigned.
1770 July 2	David Sutcliffe, in orders before 1775.
1782	—— Houghton.
,,	Matthew Moss, died about 1799.
1813	—— Sutcliffe ; afterwards Curate of Darton, under Mr. Wilkinson, and Master of Barnsley School.
181.	Joseph Edwards ; afterwards a Master in King's College School, London.

N.B.—There was no Usher appointed by the Governors for many years, Mr. Wilkinson receiving the whole Income and choosing and paying Assistants at his pleasure, so that it is doubtful whether the two preceding were really Ushers. In 1840, the Governors resumed their rights, which they exercised until the Scheme of the Endowed Schools Commission

* Grammar Schools were generally provided with two Masters, technically called 'The Master' and 'The Usher'. The latter had half the pay of the former, but the tenure of office was the same in both cases. I have never been able to trace the latter office to its origin. It was evidently well established at the time of the Reformation. The word itself is of ecclesiastical origin, but there seems a confusion of two words *Hostiarius* (a person who provided the bread for the *Hostia*) and *Ostiarius* (a person who kept the *Ostium* or door); the one has supplied the French *Huissier*, the other the English *Usher*. In schools, it denoted the Master, who had the charge of the younger pupils, sometimes called the *Petties* or *Pettites*, and taught them the Latin Grammar. At Heath School, the Usher was appointed by the Governors, who, however, had to consult the Master as to his fitness for the post.

† Richard Sterne in one of his letters in 1727 says " One Mr. Abraham Milner, a petty Schoolmaster, was concerned in getting subscriptions " for the new Charter. I find in P.R. the following:—

Married 1740, Jan. 8 { Abrm. Milner Schoolmaster and Mary Fielding Hal. Spr.

Buried 1748, Aug. 28 { Abm. Milner Hal. Bookseller and Mary Milner his Wife.

came into operation, from which time the appointment and dismissal of all Assistant Masters rest with the Head Master.

Date of appointment.			
1840	Feb. 7.	William Augustus Marsh,	B.A. Pembroke Coll. Camb.
1841	Jan.	Rev. Joshua Waltham,	B.A. St. John's ,, ,,
,,	Nov. 26.	John Gooch,	B.A. Caius ,, ,,
1843	Jan. 30.	William Henry Parr,	B.A. Catherine Hall ,,
1844	July 24.	Charles Wilmot Hardy,	B.A. Trinity Coll. ,,
1849	Jan. 8.	Frederick Russell,	B.A. ,, ,, ,,
1850	July 12.	William Kirby,	B.A. Jesus ,, ,,
1852	Jan. 19.	David Bellamy,	B.A. Catherine Hall ,,
1857	Feb. 5.	John William Earnshaw,	B.A. ,, ,, ,,
1859	Jan. 31.	Edward Carter,	B.A. New Coll. Oxfd.
1861	Sept. 18.	John Cox Edwards,	B.A. Emmanuel Coll. Camb.
1862	Oct. 20.	William Chantler Whitehead,	B.A. St. John's ,, ,,
1864	Aug.	James Mayo,	B.A. Trinity ,, ,,
1865	Jan. 2.	William John Brookes	

The Office of Usher ceased to exist in 1876 on the resignation of Mr. Brookes. The following Assistant Masters have been appointed since the New Scheme came into operation :—

1875	Jan.	William Edward Sadd,	B.A. St. Catherine's Coll. Camb.
1876	Sept.	Henry Robert Field Canham,	B.A. St. John's ,, ,,
1878	Dec. 30.	Joseph Clayton,	B.A. Emmanuel ,, ,,

3. SPECIAL EXAMINERS APPOINTED BY THE GOVERNORS.

1866 Rev. Hugh George Robinson, M.A. (Hon. Canon of York and late Principal of the Training College, York.)

1867 Rev. George Ash Butterton, D.D. (formerly Master of Uppingham and Giggleswick Gramr. Schools.)

1868 Rev. H. G. Robinson, M.A.

1869 } Rev. J. T. B. Landon, M.A. (formerly Fellow of Magdalen College,
1870 } Oxford.)

1871 } George Heppel, M.A. (St. John's Coll. Camb., late Principal of Nelson
1872 } College, New Zealand.)

1873 Rev. J. T. B. Landon, M.A.

1874 (No special Examiner.)

1875 }
1876 } George Heppel, M.A.
1877 }

1878 Rev. Joseph Schofield, B.A.

1879 R. H. Elliott, M.A.

CHAPTER XII.

§1. CELEBRATED SCHOLARS TO 1789.

§2. SCHOLARS UNDER MR. WILKINSON.

§3. COMPLETE LIST OF SCHOLARS FROM 1840 TO 1879.

§4. SCHOLARS WHO HAVE GRADUATED SINCE 1840.

§5. SCHOLARS WHO HAVE PASSED THE OXFORD AND
CAMBRIDGE LOCAL EXAMINATIONS SINCE 1861.

§1. IT is very likely that each Master would keep a private record of his pupils, but no public register has ever been provided. We consequently do not know who were scholars, or whether any ever became distinguished, with two or three exceptions. There must, however, have been many such, to induce the petitioners for a renewal of the Charter in 1726 to say "that the School had flourished for a great many. years next after its foundation, to the great benefit of the inhabitants of the parish and vicarage".

Mr. Byrron, the second Master, speaks of Dr. Favour's children being taught by him and the Usher. These would be John (born Feb. 1598-9) and William (born July 1601); the former of whom became a Prebendary of Southwell and of Ripon, and Rector of Sutton-on-Derwent and Rainton.

Mr. Cockman, the third Master, had two celebrated pupils, John Lake*, who became Vicar of Leeds, and Bishop of Man, Bristol, and Chichester in succession; and John

---

* He was born on Dec. 5th, 1624, in Petticoat Lane, now Russell St., Halifax. He went to St. John's College, Cambridge, when only thirteen years of age. He was one of the celebrated seven Bishops who resisted James II, though he afterwards became a Non-juror. He died Aug. 30th, 1689. His father, Thomas Lake, was Church-warden in 1639. His name is in Vicar Ramsden's List of subscriptions towards the endowment of the School in 1635, for 6s. 8d.

Milner*, who also became Vicar of Leeds. These were brothers-in-law, Milner marrying a sister of Lake. There was also a third pupil of Mr. Cockman, Samuel Stancliffe, who went to St. John's College, Cambridge. His name is still kept in recollection by a tablet commemorating his bequest of £100 for adorning the School†.

Mr. Lister, the seventh Master, must have the honour of having found out the genius of Laurence Sterne, if tradition is to be depended on, though he could hardly have educated him.

Mr. Ogden, the eleventh Master, was in office, while Jesse Ramsden‡, one of the most celebrated makers of mathematical instruments that England ever produced was at the School. He could not, however, have received much benefit from it, though he was a pupil for three years, as he left when twelve years of age.

It is probable that Joah Bates, who became Fellow of King's College, Cambridge, and M.A., and was afterwards a Commissioner in the Civil Service, and Henry Bates§, Fellow of Peterhouse and D.D., received their education in

---

* He was born in Feb., 1627-8, in Skircoat. He went to Christ's College, Cambridge, when about fourteen years of age. He became Vicar of St. John's, Leeds, in 1662 ; and of the Parish Church there in 1677. Being a non-juror, he resigned in 1689, and resided at St. John's College, Cambridge, until his death in Feb., 1702-3, employing his time in writing learned books.

† We might have expected Abp. Tillotson to have been at the School, as his father lived only about three miles off, and in 1635 subscribed 5s. towards the Endowment fund. He is said to have been educated at Colne.

‡ He was born at Salterhebble in September, 1731. He married the daughter of the celebrated Dollond, for whom he had done a great deal of work. He improved the Theodolite, Pyrometer, Barometer, Micrometer, &c., and invented the Dividing Machine. He became F.R.S. in 1786, and died Nov. 5th, 1800.

§ These two were sons of Henry Bates, who was appointed Parish Clerk of Halifax in 1735. Joah was a celebrated musician, and conducted the Handel Commemoration in Westminster Abbey in 1784. These two brothers together with an Oxford Graduate, and three Cambridge students, took part in the performance of the Messiah on the opening of the New Organ in Halifax Parish Church in 1766. The celebrated Herschel (father of Sir John Herschel) played the Organ. *(L.P. CIII.)*

85

the School under Mr. Ogden, and his successor, Mr. West. Major Cartwright, one of the earlier advocates of Parliamentary Reform, is said to have been at the School about this time. I am told also that one Abraham Thomas was at the School about 1735. It shews how closely we are connected with the past, when Mr. John Thomas, the present Parish Clerk of Halifax, his great-nephew, who was born in 1804, has heard him speak of his times. Abraham Thomas died in 1822, in the hundredth year of his age.

Carlisle, in his "Endowed Grammar Schools", mentions Dr. Cyril Jackson, Dean of Christ Church, Oxford, and Dr. William Jackson*, Bishop of Oxford, as having been educated at this School; but, if so, they could have been there only in their earliest days, as their biographers say that they received their education at Westminster School; and Carlisle himself also includes them among the celebrated Scholars of Manchester School. Mr. West would have been Master in their time, as they were born in 1746 and 1750 respectively.

Carlisle also mentions among the celebrated scholars "Rev. Edward Ellis, M.A., Second Master of Westminster School (appointed in 1814), and Rev. —— Sharpe†, then Vicar of Wakefield". These might have been under Mr. Kempson, or Mr. Wilkinson.

Dr. Lonsdale, Bishop of Lichfield from 1843 to 1867, was at Heath School from 1794, when only six years of age, to 1799, and then went to Eton.

---

* They were the sons of Cyril Jackson, M.D., of Stamford, who married the widow of William Rawson, Lord of the Manor of Shipley, who died in 1745. She was named Judith Prescott before marrying into the family of the Rawsons of Bradford, and was either a Prescott of Halifax by birth or the widow of a Prescott. Cyril Jackson resided in or near Halifax, as he was nominated a Governor of the School in 1753, but declined the office. He was also one of the Trust for carrying out the Halifax Water-works Act, passed in 1762. The Apothecary's Ledger, mentioned under "Mr. Lister", shews there was a Dr. Jackson in Halifax before 1700, so that Dr. Cyril Jackson was possibly connected with Halifax by birth.
† i. e., Samuel Sharp, who was instituted Vicar, Feb. 3rd, 1810.

§2. SCHOLARS UNDER MR. WILKINSON.

I have about 150 names copied from the old School Dictionaries, on the pages of which they were scribbled in school-boy fashion, many of them having most absurd dates attached. I copy those which have seemingly correct dates. N.B. * after a name means " Graduated at a University ".

1807	Ben. Gott.	1818	J. Edwards.*
1809	A. Seymour.	,,	T. Lister.
1810 (16)	J. Bebb.	,,	Tom Robson.
,,	J. Bragg.	,,	S. Watson.
,,	J. Ferrand Dearden.	1819	H. B. Cardwell.
,, (12,20)	T. Finch.*	,,	J. Dunderdale.
,,	W. T. Goodall.	,,	T. M. Gorst*.
,,	S. Walker.	,,	—— Hunt.
1811	F. Peile.	,,	C. Mayer.
1812 (13)	G. Bentley.	1820	John R. Booth.
,,	Joshua Ingham.	,,	James Farrar.
,,	F. Ingram.	,,	E. Sanderson.
,,	James Moore.	,,	W. Wainhouse.
,,	T. F. Sutcliffe.	1821	R. Wainhouse.
,,	John Tuley.	1823 (25,26)	Matthew Hy. Greenup.
1814	William Craven,	,,	W. Sanderson.
	West House, Manchester.	,,	W. Smith.
1815 (16,18)	G. Dawson.	1824	J. Ashworth*, Elland Bank.
,,	W. Hirst.	,,	J. Bailey.
,,	George Mercer.	,,	D. Edleston.
,,	Frederick Tucker.	,,	J. Jowett.
1816	Joah Crossley.*	,,	J. H. Tootal.
,,	G. Stansfeld.*	,, (20)	Thomas Watson.
,,	R. Stansfeld, Field House.	1825	R. H. Broadhurst.
1817 (19,23)	H. Foster.	,,	R. C. Hurt.
,,	W. A. Holroyde.	,,	R. Roughton.
,,	G. Marriott.	,, (29)	R. Tucker.
,,	J. Bradley Mellor.	1826	Joshua Ingham.
,,	M. Mitton.	,, (27,28)	F. Ingram.
1817 (18)	John Rawson.	,,	T. Parkinson.
,,	W. Warde.*	,, (28)	J. Sanderson.

1826	S. Stead.	1829	W. C. Stead.
,,	G. Sutcliffe.	,,	John Wild.
,,	J. Wainhouse.	1831 (37,38)	Frank Stead.
1827	David Balmforth, Stainland.	1833	S. (or T.) G. Booth.
,,	J. Broadhurst	1834	T. P. Rawson.
,,	E. Dyson.	1837	Alex. S. Hill.
,,	James Moore.	1838	J. R. Casson.
,,	B. Stocks.*	,,	Lewis Kenny.*
1828	Thomas Lambert.	,,	G. Peel.
,,	B. Milner.	,,	C. E. Priestlen.
1829	James Hiley.	,,	John Rawson, Greenroyd.

In addition to the above, I have been enabled by the kindness of some gentlemen, who were formerly pupils of the School, to make up the following List. The date to the left of the name denotes some one year or more in which the pupil was at the School; *after the name shews that he went to a University; f means "Fellow". Names within [   ] are also in the first List.

1817   Abbott, John, a name perpetuated by "The Abbott Scholarships" at Oxford and Cambridge, and "The Abbott's Home" at Halifax.

      Alcock, ——— (of Skipton), late of the Craven Bank.

      Ashworth*, Arthur Howard, (of Elland), afterwards Minor Canon of York.

1832   [Ashworth*, John Ashworth],   ,,   late f B.N.C. Oxford, and now Rector of Didcot.

      Ashworth*, Philip Sidney   '   ,,

      Ashworth, Wheelhouse   ,,

1833   Atkinson*, William   ,,   late Curate of Elland.

      (and some brothers).

181.   Baker*, Robert, afterwards Rector of Hargrave.

181.   Bates*, Thomas, afterwards Curate of Trinity Church, Halifax.

1812   [Bentley, G.]

1814   (and three others).

1830   Two Bentleys, from neighbourhood of Huddersfield.

1810   Birtwhistle, William, late surgeon at Skipton.

1810   [Bragg, J.]

181.   Bragg, Raisbeck

      Bragg, ———

1810   Bromhead*, Charles Ffrench, afterwards ƒ Trin : Coll : Cambridge.

      Brook, ——— (of Huddersfield).

      Buckley, (three from Saddleworth).

1810   Bushby*, Edward, formerly ƒ St. John's Coll : Cambridge.

      Candler, ——— (of York).

1823   Cartwright*, John, late of Durham.

1818   Charlesworth*, Beedam.

1818   Charnock*, Thomas Brooksbank.

1808   Crabtree*, ———, formerly ƒ University Coll :, Oxford.

1815   Crabtree*, James, (a younger brother).

1818   Crossley, James, late President of the Cheetham Society, Manchester.

1828   Crossley*, Joah

182.   Crossley, John, late of Manor Heath, Halifax.

1818   Dearden*, James (of Rochdale).

181.   Duffin, ——— (of Edinburgh).

1819   Dyson, John Daniel, late Colonel 3rd Dragoon Guards.

      [Dyson, Edwards]

      Dyson, George, late Coroner.

      Dyson, Thomas

      (and one other at least)

1824   [Edleston, D.]

1834   Edleston*, Joseph, D.D. late ƒ Trin : Coll : Cambridge, and now Vicar of Gainford.

182.   Edleston, T. H.

1810   Edwards, Henry, afterwards a Solicitor in London.

1809   Edwards*, Joseph, late a Master in King's Coll : School, London.

1811   Edwards, Richard

1808—20 Finch*, Thomas, now of Morpeth.

1816   Foster, John (of Heptonstall).

1810   Franks*, James Clarke (of Sowerby Bridge), late Vicar of Hudderfield. He gained the Norrisian Prize, the Members' Prize, and three times the Hulsean Prize at Cambridge.

1830   Garlick, ——— ⎫
                  ⎬ not brothers.
1830   Garlick, ——— ⎭

      Gillmor, William (of Illingworth), son of the late Vicar.

1820   Gorst, Edward Chadock, afterwards a solicitor at Preston.

1819   [Gorst*, Thomas Mee]

1813   Greenwood*, William, ƒ Corpus Christi Coll : Cambridge.

181.   Hall*, Edward

1815   Hall*, Robert, late M.P. for Leeds, and Recorder of Hull.

181.   Hall, Stephen, afterwards a solicitor at Skipton.

181.   Harrison, J., now a surgeon at Chester

183 .   Hebden, W. H.
1828   Hiley, John
1830   Hiley*, Simeon (of Elland), late ƒ St. John's Coll : Cambridge.
1837   [Hill, Alexander Staveley], now M.P. for Coventry.
1817   [Holroyde, W. A.]
         (and two others).
1810   Hopper, ———
1816   Horsfall, Timothy
1816   Huntriss, William, (now of Westfield, Halifax).
1829   Ikin, ———, late Town-clerk of Leeds (?)
1818   Ingham*, James Taylor, (of Mirfield), now Sir James, a London Police
         . Magistrate.
1821   Kellett, Henry
1838   [Kenny*, Lewis Stanhope, now Rector of Kirkby-Knowle.]
183 .   Kenny, William Fenton, afterwards a solicitor at Halifax.
1810   Lambert, John (of Elland).
1818   Lambert, Robert (of Elland).
1836   Lewthwaite*, Samuel, late ƒ Magdalene Coll : Cambridge.
1794—99 Lonsdale*, John, late ƒ King's Coll : Cambridge, and Bishop of Lichfield.
1814   Mc.Bean, William
1829—1835 Mallinson*, Whiteley, now Vicar of Cross-stone, late ƒ Magdalene
         Coll : Cambridge.
1818   Maude*, Daniel, late ƒ of Caius Coll : Cambridge, and a London Police
         Magistrate.
1818   Maude*, Frank, late Vicar of Hoyland.
1818   Maude*, Ralph, late Vicar of Mirfield.
1820   Milnes, ———
1814   Mitchell, John Herbert
1823   Moore, William
1810   Newall, Noel, (of Littleborough).
1813   Newman, Edward, now a Solicitor at Barnsley.
1803   Newman, William, late of Darley Hall.
1814   Norris, Charles
1814   Norris*, James
1814   Norris, Sidney
1832   Nussey*, ——— (fr. Derbyshire).
181 .   Oxley, R., late M.D. at Pontefract.
179 .   Pollard, George
1818   Pollard, James (of Manchester)
181 .   Priestley, Charles (of White Windows, near Halifax),
181 .   Priestley, George
181 .   Priestley, Henry

182 . Ramsden, ——
182 . Ramsden, ——
1813 Rawson, Edward (of the Shay)
1813 Rawson, John (of the Shay).
179 . Rhodes, J. A.
1813 Rhodes, William
182 . Richardson, (of Southowram),
181 . Rishworth, ——, afterwards a Banker at Wakefield.
       Rothwell, John
1825 Roughton, John
       Royds, Albert
1816 Royds*, Charles
1816 Scot, ——, afterwards M.D. at Liverpool.
1816 Scot, ——, (one of these was named Roger).
1815 Serjeantson, Charles (of York),
       Settle, Robert, afterwards an attorney at Halifax.
1810 Shaw*, Edward Butterworth
181 . Shaw, George, afterwards M.D. at Leicester.
1830 Slater, Joseph (of Elland).
183 . Slater, ———— (brother of Joseph)
1834 Smith*, William Ramsden, late Vicar of Christ Church, Bradford.
183 . Sowden*, Sutcliffe
1818 [Stansfeld*, George]
1818 Stansfeld*, John
1816 [Stansfeld, Robert], Hony. Col. 6th West York Militia.
1810 Staveley, Henry (?)
1810 Staveley, James
1810 Staveley, John
179 . Stead, John
1827 [Stocks*, Benjamin]
1813 Stocks, George, afterwards a surgeon in Blackburn
       Stocks, Joseph
1815 Stocks, Michael
181 . Sunderland*, Thomas
181 . Tennant, Philip
1818 Tennant*, Sanderson
       (and three others).
1818 Tong, W.
1815 Turner, Benjamin (from India).
1810 Turney, John, late of Leek Wotton near Warwick.
1823—30 [Wainhouse, John Edward]

1817   Walsh, Thomas Selby, afterwards Mayor of Halifax.
1817   [Warde*, William], afterwards Vicar of Witton-le-wear.
1818   Watson*, Charles
       Watson*, T. C.
       Watson, Shipley, afterwards M.D. at York.
1819   Whiteley, Thomas
1817   Wilson*, ———— (of York)
1818   Wright, Edward

§3.   COMPLETE LIST OF SCHOLARS FROM 1840 TO 1879.

Mr. Gooch and Mr. Cox have both kept private Registers, from which the following names are taken in the order of their admission.

Admitted by MR. GOOCH.

1840 Aug.	Gooch, Charles	1840 Aug.	Kenny, Lewis Stanhope
	Holroyd, John Bailey		Casson, William John
	Norris, Henry Alexander		Foster, William Mitchell
	Norris, William Arthur		Jellicorse, Edward John
	Barker, Frederic		Brown
	Priestley, William		Ewing, Alexander
	Smith, Robert Harman		Hirst, Henry Alexander
	Dew, John Wormald		Dowson, Edward Withers
	Dew, Croft Worgan		Barlow, John
	Akers, Edward		Catley, Edwin
	Holdsworth, Tom		Alexander, Henry Hamerton
	Holdsworth, John	Sept.	Wolstenholme, Edward
	Beck, William		Parker
	Speight, Thomas	Oct.	McNeill, Malcolm
	Speight, John	Nov.	Hague, William Drake
	Eastwood, John William	1841 Feb.	Haigh, William
	Eastwood, Thomas		Haigh, George Henry
	Eastwood, Charles James		Whiteley, Robert
	Peel, Lawrence		Ogden, William
	Mercer, Isaac		Riley, George
	Gaukroger, Joseph		Thornton, John Varley

92

1841 Mar.	Ambler, James Pearson	1843 July	Turner, Joseph
April	Sowden, George		Smith, Walter
July	Ogden, John	Oct.	Dew, George Platt
	Beck, Robert	1844 Jan.	Crossley, Edward
	Beaumont, Thomas George	Mar.	Cash, John
	Jackson, Thomas Riley	April	Emmet, William Henry
	Priestley, Charles Edwards	1845 Jan.	Baines, George
	Hirst, Samuel Henry		Beaumont, Butterworth
	Hirst, Edward Smith	Feb.	Rogers, Thomas Henry
	Stansfield, Samuel		Brierly, Alfred
	Stansfield, Thomas	April	Whittaker, Charles
	Stansfield, Joseph Hudson	Aug.	Davis, John Edward
	Hanson, Joseph		Goodall, William Tatham
	Foster, Henry		Cormick, Richard
Sept.	Stead, Joseph	1846 Jan.	Hill, John Edwards
	Stead, Richard William	Feb.	Oates, James Daniel
	Stead, James	April	Ingham, Samuel
	Crowther, John Brown	May	Good, James
Oct.	Roberts, John	July	Norris, Sidney Perfect
	Drake, George Vandyke		Stocks, Joseph Halliday
1842 Jan.	Emmet, Charles		Hammerton, Stephen
	Garnet, Henry Eli		Edward Nelson
	Barstow, William	Oct.	Hamerton, Ernest
	Lewthwaite, Joseph		Hamerton, Joseph
	Norris, Charles Musgrave	1847 Feb.	Crossley, John Edward
Feb.	Wrigley, Watts Henry		Booth, John Robinson
April	Norris, Francis John		Booth, Thomas George
	Stead, William Charles	Mar.	Taylor, Alfred
	Kenny, Alfred John		Fox, Joseph
	Sugden, ( )		Baines, Simpson
July	Oldfield, James	April	Walker, Richard Henry
	Wood, Charles	Aug.	Rouse, Edward Peake
	Royston, Thomas	1848 Jan.	Pitchforth, Aquila
	Midgley, Francis		Garlick, John William
	Ward, William Mann	Feb.	Wood, Henry
	Baker, Robert Sibley		Wood, William
1843 Jan.	Rouse, John		Wood, Richard S.
Mar.	Hirst, James	Mar.	Bairstow, Thomas
July	Turney, Thomas Henry	April	Riley, Edwin
	Turney, Benjamin	July	Swallow, John Henry
	Hurst, John		Swallow, Thomas Dawson

1818		Hammerton, Robert
		Chisenhall
	July	Walker, Samuel
		Smith, Charles Henry
		Dyson, John Charles
	Aug.	Nelson, Tom
		Binns, Wildon
		Binns, Cornelius
		Outram, Edmund
	Oct.	Law, Joseph Henry
1849	Jan.	Wright, Alfred William
		Holroyde, Walter James
	April	Bayldon, Joe Wood
		Lees, Thomas Lister
	Aug.	Fox, Charles James
		Bulmford, David
		Highley, Thomas Sutcliffe
		Turner, ( )
		Garlick, Henry Grainger
		Earnshaw, John William
		Pickles, Jonas
		Eastwood, Henry
		Nicholson, Thomas
		Farrer, Thomas Henry
		Hobson, George
		Macaulay, Francis Edwin
	Oct.	Gardiner, Henry Walter
1850	Jan.	Edgar, Donald
		Ingham, Richard
		Orange, Wm. Alexander
		Wildman
		Stainburn, George
		Swallow, George Edward
		Ellam, Ralph Bate
	Feb.	Remington, Frederick Hardy
		Garside, Joseph
	April	Brown, James Laurie
		Wilson, Alfred Henry
		Shaw, Benjamin Walker
		Macaulay, Charles
		Stansfield, William Farrar

1850	July	Clegg, Wesley
	Aug.	Wright, John Armstrong
		Paterson
		Highley, Oliver
		Highley, Arthur
		Walton, Keighley
		Winstanley, Calvin
		Beaumont
		Camm, John Brooke Maher
		Adamson, Charles
		Knowles, George
		Slater, Joseph Henry
		Sidebottom, Cuthbert Gerald
	Sep.	Holroyd, George Gomersall
		Highley, Charles
	Oct.	Hirst, William
		Holroyd, Sutcliffe
1851	Feb.	Dearden, Frederick
		Dearden, Thomas
		Bottomley, Lawrence
		Whinray
		Crowther, Frederick
		Dearden, William
	Mar.	Caw, John
	April	Hindson, John Sanderson
		Smith
		Rawson, Thomas Preston
	Aug.	Bottomley, William Henry
	Sep.	Tillotson, Arthur
	Oct.	Fell, Joseph
		Crapper, Foster
		Simpson, John William
		Simpson, Frederick
		Rouse, William Archibald
1852	Jan.	Storey, Walter
		Maude, William
		Davies, James Heywood
		Swallow, Joseph
		Stott, Thomas Dean
	Feb.	Busfeild, William
		Busfeild, John

1852 Feb. Busfeild, Currer Fothergill
Bedford, Robert Thomas
April Booth, John Whitley
Aug. Foster, Alfred ·
Campbell, James Thomas
Goodall, Alfred
Smith, Solomon Charles
Smith, Edward James
Orange, John Edward
Sep. Fleming, Walter
Oct. Rawnsley, Albert
Nov. Scott, William
Scott, John
1853 Feb. Hoadley, Robert
Fox, William
Boddy, John William
Burton, Charles Harryfred
Helliwell, Thomas William
Eastwood, Joseph
Dyson, Rowland
Hadfield, William
Green, Thomas Foulds
Horsfall
Briggs, William Rawdon
Shaw, William
Rawson, Charles Collinson
Higham, Joseph
Mar. Steele, Alexander Denton
April Woodhouse, Randal
Robinson, Richard Henry
Aug. Charnock, James Hanson
Crapper, Walter
Smallwood, George
Smallwood, John Casson
Laycock, George Diggs
Laycock, William
Laycock, Samuel F.
Sutcliffe, Charles
Oct. Blackburn, Henry
Barstow, Charles,
Baines, Joseph Mellor

1854 Feb. Gresley, Charles
Taylor, Charles
Walker, John William
Bairstow, James Oates
Foster, Alfred
Blagbrough, Walter
Walker, Samuel
Robinson, Frederick William
Hey, David
Thwaite, Christopher
Thwaite, Edward Hall
Frobisher, Frederick
Mar. Skelton, Matthew Henry
Aspinall, George Edward
Emmet, George Edward
Pitts, Thomas
April Cockroft, Herbert
Aug. Hirst, Thomas Henry
Franklin, Harry
Sutcliffe, Thomas
Hitchen, Charles Whiteley
Prescott, John Barrow
Prescott, Cyril Jackson
Clark
Smith, Charles Frederick
Dyer, Francis William
Sep. Prest, John Cooper
Oct. Mallinson, John Ralph
Rhodes, Christopher Tate
Crossley, Joseph
Nov. Emmet, Charles Edward
1855 Jan. Kershaw, John Edward
Mellor, William Wood
Feb. Walker, Thomas Ibbetson
Smith, Jonathan
Eastwood, Henry
Eastwood, Samuel
Tomlin, Ottiwell
April Hawkyard, Benjamin
Kenny, Courtney Stanhope
Aug. Staveley, Arkyl John Arthur

1855 April	Korshaw, William	
	Child, William Hall	
	Norris, Charles Edwin	
	Norris, Wallace Lea	
	Emmet, Joseph Alfred	
	Walker, Charles John	
Sep.	Lambert, John	
Oct.	Hudson, Charles	
	Mitchell, John Herbert	
1856 Jan.	Alexander, Arthur William	
Feb.	Turner, Thomas	
April	Mc. Clure, John	
Aug.	Barrowby, John	
	Bowman, Henry Hearder	
	Greenwood, Sidney	
	Mitchell, William Henry	
	Highley, Joe	
	Smith, Samuel Vincent	
Sep.	Elliott, James	
1857 Jan.	Illingworth, John Blow	
	Patchett, John	
	Patchett, Frank	
	Robinson, Henry	
	Sutcliffe, John	
Feb.	Alexander, Reginald Gervase	
	Barraclough, Arthur	
	Parsons, John M.	
	Parsons, Edwin	
	Holyday, Charles William	
Mar.	Smith, Sidney	
Aug.	Foster, William	
	Sutcliffe, Thomas	
	Parsons, Oswald	
	Kitchen, Martin Mauley	
Sep.	Thomas, Joseph	
Oct.	Mallinson, Benjamin	
1858 Feb.	Clemesha, Robert John	
	Fox, John	
Mar.	Pitts, Bernard	
April	Hall, John William	
Aug.	Huntriss, William	
	Huntriss, Edward	
	Swallow, Richard Dawson	

1858 Aug.	Shaw, John Edward	
	Bean, Alexander Henry	
	Bennett, Edward Robinson	
	Rhodes, Arthur	
	Rhodes, Godfrey	
	Warren, Edward Walpole	
	Coates, George	
1859 Feb.	Morris, Thomas Henry	
	Sutcliffe, John	
	Broadbent, John Henry	
	Dunderdale, William James	
	Dunderdale, Thomas	
April	Norris, Priestley	
Aug.	Caw, Arthur Worgan	
	Caw, Herbert Kenyon	
	Claybrough, John Fletcher	
	Henrey, Joseph	
	Henrey, William M.	
1860 Feb.	Hill, Walter	
	Jennings, Walter Milton	
	Swallow, James Edward	
Mar.	Kershaw, Henry Walter	
April	Town, Robert Samuel	
	Pollit, Charles Thomas	
	Masheder, Thomas	
	Nuttall, Lawrence	
Aug.	Smithies, John Fox	
	Norris, Henry Percy	
	Rawson, Benjamin Currer	
	Coates, William Charles	
	Lepper, Charles Harper	
Sept.	Stephenson, Thomas	
	Bilborough	
Oct.	Mallinson, William	
1861 Jan.	Buxton, George	
Feb.	Ingram, Richard Francis	
	Ingram, James Hughes	
	Appleton	
Aug.	Empsall, Samuel	
	Huntriss, William James	
	Huntriss, Frederick George	
	Smithies, William Edward	
	Snow, Thomas Collins	

Admitted by MR. COX.

1861 Oct.	Fletcher, Robert Crompton	1863 Jan.	Patchett, James
	Irvin, John Spendlove		Patchett, Riley
	Seed, Thomas		Smith, Arthur William
	Seed, John	Feb.	Nicklin, John William
	Barnes, Francis Joshua		Dow, Andrew Munro
	Pritt, Thomas Evan	April	Newton, George Alfred
	Kirby, Christopher John	Aug.	Garside, Herbert
	Walsh, Alfred Ramsden		Duncan, Robert Leyland
	Wright, Robert Hood		Farnell, James
	Kirk, Joseph Moxon		Stansfeld, Raywood
Nov.	Whitworth, Joseph Whitely		Micklethwaite
1862 Jan.	Sandford, Edward Armitage		Stansfeld, George
	Sandford, Henry Rossall		Palethorpe, Henry John
	Common, James	Oct.	Seed, William Henry
	Cliff, Arthur Foster		Bonser, John Winfield
	Mallinson, William Crowther		Gaukroger, Frederic
	Farrar, Edward		Mitchell
	Hebblethwaite, Samuel	1864 Jan.	Tasker, John William
	Common, Arthur Welsh		Taylor, Alfred Henry Smith
	Dempster, Robert		Oates, Walter Holroyd
	Sutcliffe, Francis Edgar		Brown, John Fisher
	Bull, Henry Beach	Feb.	Priestley, Frederick
	Maud, William Wade		Sutcliffe, Tom
	Hebblethwaite, George		Gaukroger, George William
	Farrar, Walter	Aug.	Fawcett, Joseph
April	Atkinson, Nelson Aaron		Crowther, Allen
	Aspinall, John		Mallinson, Arthur
Aug.	Robinson, Herbert		Kershaw, Frederick William
	Whitworth, William		Robinson, Herbert
	Mitchell, John		Mathias, Bennett Seymour
	Jeffery, Samuel	Oct.	Lewthwaite, Joseph
Sep.	De Tivoli, Giuseppe		Macdonald, James Alexander
Oct.	Slingsby, Frederick William		Donald John
	Maude, John	1865 Jan.	Fleming, George
1863 Jan.	Price, Charles	Feb.	Nuttall, Fred
	Price, William	Mar.	Granger, Henry Thomas
	Alexander, John Barrow		Granger, Thomas Colpotts
	Murray, Archiebald Stavert	April	Robinson, George William

97

1865 May — Bland, William Edward Joseph; Wynn, Frederick Arthur; Swallow, Frederick; Firth, Henry Williams; Bailey, William; Parker, Thomas Henry; Fleming, Albert
1866 Jan. — Livy, Frederic Young; Salmond, David Norman; Brierley, Frederick William
Feb. — Whitworth, Robert; Lupton, John Edward
Aug. — Watson, Andrew; Cammack, Thomas William; Walsh, Alfred; Haigh, John William; Hoyle, George; Fleming, Edward; Robinson, Richard
Oct. — Spencer, William Isaac; Robinson, James Frederick; Cheadle, Alfred Stanley; Middlebrook, Joseph
1867 Jan. — Stott, Charles Thomas; Schofield, Simeon; Rankin, Henry Francis; Wilkinson, Henry Newstead; Ison, Henry William; Miller, Thomas James; Boothman, Edward
Feb. — Smith, Charles Edwin; Goodall, Arthur Alfred Edward
April — Holroyde, John; Willey, John; Hey, Thomas; Macdonald, Edward William Jackson; Macdonald, Roderick John Johnstone; Barker, Ralph Atkinson

1867 Aug. — Cox, Thomas Buchanan; Hunt, John Frank; Rudd, Harold; Wightman, Charles; Scholefield, John
Oct. — Tate, William; Tate, Charles; Bancroft, James; Shoesmith, Louis William Henry
1868 Jan. — Jackson, Lawrence Hartley; Gray, William; Robertshaw, James; Rhodes, Herbert Rothwell; Swallow, Herbert; Cox, Robert Stavert; Morrison, William Beamish Austin; Parkinson, Thomas; Baines, Frederick Horace; Baines, James Arthur; Berry, John William
Feb. — Booth, Charles Oldfield; Coates, Richard; Shoesmith, Denton
Aug. — Norris, Moraston Ormerod; Haigh, Charles; Kershaw, Richard; Firth, Thomas Williams; Stritch, Michael Chute; Ostler, Frederick William; Ostler, John; Ostler, William Henry
1869 Jan. — Mitchell, Thomas; Lupton, Harold Edgar; Edleston, Alfred Blakey; Heal, James Hardy
Feb. — Hodgson, Edward; Ackroyd, James Edward; Greenwood, Abraham; Hebblethwaite, James

1869 April Sowerby, John Francis
Nettleton, Arthur
Thomson, George Thomas
Coton, Frederick
Kershaw, Arthur Noble
Lockett, Charles Alfred
Mitchell, John Holroyde
Aug. Pickles, Walter
Whiteley, George
Frobisher, John
Frobisher, William
Ellison, Ernest Henry
Womersley, William Henry
Fletcher, Wilfred William
Ernest
Thompson, Frederic William
Sep. Waithman, Charles Anthony
Waithman, James Clarkson
Oct. Charlton, Harry Irlam
Haigh, Frederick William
1870 Jan. Hill, Ernest Hatton
Kippax, Smith
Palethorpe, Arthur Shackles
Warneford, Harry Launcelot
Henry, George
Wood, Frederick
Whiteley, Tom Harry
Feb. Turner, Benjamin
April Wood, John Edward
Ostler, Arthur
Taylor, William Dearnley
Aug. Jessop, Richard Henry
Naylor, Arthur
Waddington, Eli Wilkinson
Waddington, Henry
Sep. Culpan, Richard
Cousin, Albert
Oct. Hill, John Edwards
Hope, John Basil
Nov. Grime, Edward Hatton
Reynall

1871 Jan. Nicholl, Joseph
Whiteley, John Alfred
Parsons, Alfred
Clayton, Harry
Eastwood, Sam
Blackburn, Charles Henry
Blackburn, Herbert
Oxley, Frederick James
Kenny, Charles Willliam
Fenton
Snepp, John
Naylor, James Herbert
Swaine, William
Fielding, Albert
Feb. Cousin, Gaston
Dixon, Fred
Mar. Shaw, John Arthur
Ramskill, Thomas
April Whittell, Alfred
Edwards, Alfred
Wilson, Thomas
Wood, Henry Lees
Greenwood, Arthur
Aug. Crabtree, Wallace
Crabtree, Fred
Mitchell, Joseph Harger
Stott, John Henry
Dixon, Fred
Hill, Walter William
Hope, George Wilfrid
Chapman, Arthur Frederic
Booth, Edward Whitley
Ainley, George Henry
Patchett, Percy
Oldfield, Louis
Chaytor, Reginald Clervaux
Oct. Longbottom, Louis Henry
1872 Jan. Bamford, Earnest Walton
Lupton, Clement Harold
Lupton, Clifford John
Mooney, Thomas Rankin

1872 Aug.	Child, Harold Edward Akroyd	1874 Jan.	Swift, George
	Cox, Edward Samuel		Clegg, John Henry
	Wood, Arthur James		Pohlmann, Fred
	Hainsworth, Robinson		Pohlmann, Edward
	Mellor, Wilfrid Arnold	Mar.	Crossley, James
	Stott, Alfred		Riley, Thomas Herbert
	Falkingbridge, John Andrew	April	Jones, Thomas William
	Gatenby		Pickard, Edwin Walter
	Pohlmann, Arthur		Holmes, Howard Arthur
	Pohlmann, George		Moffett, John Ritchie
Oct.	Thomas, William Fletcher		Hill, Charles Marshal
	Moore, William Thomas		Street, Samuel
1873 Jan.	Swaine, Henry John		Street, Ashton
	Armstrong, Henry	Aug.	Ingham, William Crossley
	Turner, John		Blackburn, Arthur
	Wilson, Frederic William		Fox, Charles Edward
	Lewthwaite, Alfred John		Patchett, John
Mar.	Marshall, Robert		Shoesmith, John William
	Crowther, John	Oct.	Town, Theodore
	Town, William Edward	1875 Jan.	Chambers, Thomas
	Town, Arthur Henry		Milnes, Robert
	Francis, Albert Edward		Bottomley, Francis Edgar
April	Lees, James Arthur		Hope, Clement Armitage
Aug.	Snepp, Alfred Neville		Farrar, Samuel Arthur
	Snepp, Rowan Lee		Collier, Harry
	Smeeton, William Mills		Collier, John Ernest
	Smeeton, Charles Henry		Vickerman, James Edward
	Jessop, John William	Feb.	Kershaw, John Herbert
	Fox, John William	Sep.	Hoyle, Samuel
	Thomson, Charles Henry		Hoyle, John
	Lees, Albert Ernest		Midgley, Arthur Walter
	Pickles, Harry		Parker, Thomas James
	Tuley, Frank		Holmes, Walter Herbert
	Haslam, Arthur Stuart		Greame
	Hope, James Arthur	1876 Jan.	Pilcher, Arthur
Sep.	Jackson, Arthur Glenn		Holmes, Fred
1874 Jan.	Holmes, Ernest Percival		Hill, Harold
	Holmes, Cyril Lake		Cox, William Francis
	Longbottom, Arthur		Davis, John Henry Grant
	Thompson		Reid, Thomas Bernard
	Shoesmith, Edward Ernest	April	Appleyard, Scott

1876	April	Appleyard, John	1878	Jan.	Craven, Fred Morris
		Kirby, Thomas			Dawes, George Douglas
	Sep.	Davis, Francis Henry		Feb.	Stansfield, Frederick William
		Kershaw, Brunel		April	Dyson, Frank Watson
		Kershaw, John Buckley		May	Horsfall, James Herbert
	Oct.	Whitaker, Sidney Morgan		Sep.	Rouse, Charles Herbert
1877	Jan.	Wilms, Louis Armin			Cox, Richard
.		Hirst, Charles	1879	Jan.	Dewhirst, Joseph Brook
		Storey, Louis			Waghorn, Christopher
	April	Brierley, James			Brook, Edgar Deighton
		Hatton, William Douglas		April	Denison, William Ernest
	Sep.	Hooson, Evan			Stott, Ernest Herbert
		Hope, Charles Stuart			Fox, Samuel
		Firth, Sidney			Holmes, Charles Gerard
		Longbottom, Rigby Sharp			de Gorham
	Sep.	Taylor, George		Sep.	Marshall, John
	Nov.	Dawes, Francis Spearman			Ingham, Wilfrid
1878	Jan.	Woodhead, Arthur			Lockwood, James
		Clegg, Charles			Ramsden, Harry Walton
		Wright, Sam Ayrton			Rawnsley, Leonard
		Stott, Frank Charles			Riley, John

101

§4. SCHOLARS WHO HAVE GRADUATED SINCE 1840.

N.B.—' Cambridge ' is meant except otherwise stated.

B.A.	College.	Honours.	
1845 Sowden, George	Magdalene	Milner Scholar	
1846 Baker, Robert	,,	,,	
1847 Gooch, Charles	,,	,,	40th Wrangler
1847 Roberts, John	,,	,, , and Fellow	{ 39th Sen. Opt.
			{ 5th in Class I.
1847 Wolstenholme, Edward Parker	Trinity		{ 30th Wrangler
			{ 13th in Class III.
1850 Kenny. Lewis Stanhope	Trinity, Oxfd.		
1852 Dew, Croft Worgan	Jesus	S'holar	
1852 Garnet, Henry Eli	Trinity, Dublin		
1853 Ogden, William	St. John's		11th Jun. Opt.
1855 Winstanley, Calvert Beaumont	Jesus		Class I (in Law)
1855 Beaumont, Thomas George	Magdalene	Milner Scholar	{ 18th Jun. Opt.
			{ Class III.
1856 Smith, Robert Harman		,,	
1856 Stainburn, George	Trinity		
1856 Wood, William	Jesus		
1857 Earnshaw, John William	St. Catherine's	Scholar	18th Sen. Opt.
1858 Rouse, Edward Peake	Trinity	Scholar, and Fellow	10th Wrangler
1858 Bayldon, Joe Wood	Sidney		
1860 Remington, Frederic Hardy	Magdalene	Milner Scholar	
1860 Barrowby, John	St. John's		
1861 Rouse, William Archibald	Trinity	Scholar	24th Wrangler
1861 Warren, Edward Walpole	Magdalene	Milner Scholar	
1865 Pitts, Thomas	Emmanuel	Scholar, and Fellow	16th Wrangler
1870 Bonser, John Winfield	Christ's	Scholar, and Fellow	SENIOR CLASSIC
1870 1Swallow, Richard Dawson	Corpus	Scholar	
1872 1Swallow, James Edward	Jesus	Scholar	3rd in Class II.
1874 *2Snow, Thomas Collins	Corpus, Oxfd.	Scholar of Corpus ; } Fellow of St. John's. }	First Class
1874 *Mitchell, John	University, Oxfd.		Second Class in Theology
1875 1Jeffery, Samuel	Magdalene	Milner Scholar	20th in Class II.

* Snow and Mitchell did not proceed to the University directly from this School, but were pupils of it for 4½ years and 3 years respectively.

1. R. D. Swallow, J. E. Swallow, and S. Jeffery obtained also a Goldsmith's Company's Exhibition in competitive examinations.

2. Snow was also Craven University Scholar.

§5. SCHOLARS WHO HAVE PASSED THE OXFORD AND
CAMBRIDGE LOCAL EXAMINATIONS SINCE 1861.

1864	Swallow, Richard Dawson	Oxford	(Senior)	
1865	*Smith, Arthur William	,,	,,	
1867	†Jeffery, Samuel	Cambridge	(Junior)	Class I.
1868	do. do.	,,	(Senior)	Class I.
1869	Hoyle, George	Oxford	(Senior)	
1869	Robinson, George William	,,	(Junior)	
1872	Parkinson, Thomas	Cambridge	(Senior)	{ Mark of distinction in Latin.
1873	Cox, Thomas Buchanan	,,	(Junior)	
1873	Hey, Thomas	,,	,,	
1874	Cox, Thomas Buchanan	Oxford	,,	
1874	Hey, Thomas	,,	,,	
1876	Hill, Ernest Hatton	Cambridge	,,	Class III.
1877	Hoyle, John	Oxford	,,	Class III.
1877	Chambers, Thomas	Cambridge	,,	Class II.
1877	Holmes, Howard Arthur	,,	,,	Class III.
1877	Hoyle, John	,,	,,	Class III.
1878	Stott, Alfred	,,	,,	{ Class I. with a mark of distinction in both Latin & Greek.
1878	Cox, Edward Samuel	,,	,,	
1878	Francis, Albert Edward	,,	,,	
1878	Fox, Charles Edward	,,	,,	

---

* A. W. Smith also obtained the First Prize at Guy's Hospital in Classics.

† Jeffery was not in the School for a year preceding this, but had been a pupil for four years previous.

George Coates obtained by Examination in 1865 a Commission without purchase.
Henry Thomas Granger was very high in Examination for a Commission in 1868.

CHAPTER XIII.

SHORTLY before his death in 1768, Sterne wrote a short Memoir of himself, in which he says:—"The autumn "of that year [1723] or the spring afterward my father "got leave of his colonel to fix me at school, which he did "near Halifax, with an able master; with whom I staid "some time, till my cousin Sterne* of Elvington [near York] "became a father to me, and sent me to the University, "&c. &c." "My poor father died March 1731. I remained "at Halifax till about the latter end of the year, and cannot "omit mentioning this anecdote of myself, and schoolmaster. "He had the cieling of the schoolroom new whitewash'd : "the ladder remained there. I one unlucky day mounted "it, and wrote with a brush, in large capital letters, LAU. "STERNE, for which the usher severely whipped me. My "master was very much hurt at this, and said, before me, "that never should that name be effaced, for I was a boy "of genius, and he was sure I should come to preferment: "this expression made me forget the stripes I had received. "In the year thirty-two† my cousin sent me to the university, "where I staid some time".

---

* *i. e.*, the son of Richard Sterne of Woodhouse, who was the brother of Laurence's father, Roger.

† He was admitted of Jesus College, July 6th, 1733, as sizer under the tuition of Mr. Cannon. He graduated B.A. January, 1736; M.A. July, 1740.

It has always been believed that Heath School was the
place where Sterne received his education and displayed
his genius; but who first mentioned Heath in print, I have
not been able to find out. Wright and Watson in their
histories say nothing of Sterne's school or of his freak,
though the former was curate of Halifax in 1732, and the
latter succeeded him in 1750. The latter indeed says, when
speaking of Woodhouse in Copley, where Sterne's uncle,
Richard Sterne, lived :—" The Rev. Mr. Sterne, author of
Tristram Shandy &c. was of this family ". Crabtree mentions
Heath School, but gives no authority for his statement.
In a copy of Sterne's works in the Library of Mr. John
Turney*, of Leek Wotton in Warwickshire, at the foot of
the page where the anecdote is told, there occurs this note
in manuscript :—" These Letters were as Sterne wrote them
" when I was at Heath School in the Year 1809-10, since
" which time they have been effaced by a stupid Whitewasher
" who washed them out as little known to the Master of his
" day as Sterne wrote them. John Turney ".—The White-
washing seems confirmed by the Governors' account books,
which in 1811 have this entry " Jno. Edwards, Plaistering
at the School £12 3s. 6d." In a letter to Wm. Craven, Esq.,†
of Clapton Lodge, Mr. Turney writes —" The name of Sterne
" was marked on the cieling of the School Room in irregular
" Characters, as if done by some one who knew he was doing
" wrongly & was fearful of being detected in the Act. They
" were large Letters, say (I speak from memory of course) about
" 4½ inches high all Capitals. They were black as if, as I
" thought, burnt in with a Candle, the smoke from the Candle
" causing them to be black............Lau Sterne was inscribed
" about 3 yards from the Head Master's desk. It ran obliquely

---

* This gentleman died Sep. 20th, 1879.
† I am indebted to Mr. Craven for a kind communication of these particulars.

" from S. W. with rather a turn to the East*". In one of the old Dictionaries (see p. 19) there is written " L. Stearn ", which may or may not be his writing, but some branches of his family spelled the name with ' *a* ' in it. Edward Newman, Esq., Solicitor, of Barnsley, writes me thus:—" The place " where Sterne wrote his name on the Ceiling of your School " was pointed out to me when I was there in 1813. My " Brother was there too, 10 years earlier, but I never heard " him say that he saw it ". The Rev. Thomas Finch, of Morpeth, who was a pupil from 1808 to 1820, says in a letter to me, " The legend during the time that I was at Heath " respecting Sterne was that he was a scholar there, and the " panel on the ceiling was pointed out, on which he was said " to have daubed Lau : Sterne ", as if it was not there in his time.

One would think that the tradition was satisfactorily confirmed. If the act was done, it must have been done before 1727, for in the latter part of that year the Master was superannuated, and therefore before Sterne was 14 years of age, or after March 1730-1, when he was in his eighteenth year. It does not seem likely that he would then have been whipped by an Usher. There is however a serious contradiction between Sterne's statement and the facts which we have mentioned in a former Chapter. Sterne speaks of an "able Master". Now Mr. Lister had in 1723 been already Master 35 years, and a contemporary says, on his death in 1728, that there had not been a rightly-qualified Master for nearly 40 years, and describes the Master as a good-for-naught fellow. In seems singular also that in 1727 Sterne's Uncle with his newly appointed fellow-governors " proceeded (as he says) to examine into the School " and

---

* The ceiling was carefully washed and examined when the old building was taken down in 1879, but no trace of the inscription was found.

found among other things "the present Master to be superannuated, the Usher about 19 or 20, and, no doubt, a person
far from being capable of discharging his duty". This
to the Archbishop, but a few days before in a letter to the
Vicar he says, that the scholars to their great loss had for
many years been neglected. How then could any one who had
been a pupil at the time say that he had been under an able
Master? Laurence was perhaps acquainted with Mr. Lister,
and had him in mind when describing the pedagogue which
Mr. Shandy would not have for his son. At any rate we
know that the persons of his tale were most, if not all,
persons whom he had met with during his life. The reader
will feel that the writer satirises somebody when he thus
writes:—"The governor I make choice of shall neither lisp
"or squint or talk loud or look fierce or foolish; or bite
"his lips or grind his teeth or speak through his nose or
"pick it, or blow it with his fingers".

"He shall neither walk fast, or slow, or fold his arms,
"for that is laziness; or hang them down, for that is folly;
"or hide them in his pocket, for that is nonsense. He
"shall neither strike or pinch or tickle, or bite or cut his
"nails or hawk or spit or snift or drum with his feet or
"fingers in company. I will have him cheerful facete jovial;
"at the same time prudent attentive to business, vigilant,
"acute argute inventive quick in resolving doubts and
"speculative questions; he shall be wise and judicious and
"learned". (Tristram Shandy, c. 48.) Verily Sterne must
have met with some queer Schoolmasters!

Sterne evidently had a poor memory for dates at any
rate. He did not remember whether he went to school in
the autumn of 1723 or the following spring; he misdated
his entrance into the University; nor would anyone from
his own statement think that he stayed there long enough

to take a degree. Whether he learned anything under his able Master, is uncertain. At any rate it is said that "he would learn when he pleased and not oftener than once a fortnight". (*Fitzgerald's Life of Sterne, p.* 87.)

I should never have questioned the tradition relating to his school, had it not been said that he was fixed at Hipperholme and not at Heath. Mr. Lister, of Shibden Hall, tells me that Miss Lister, who is now alive and about 80 years of age, says she distinctly remembers her father telling her that Laurence Sterne used to walk to Hipperholme School from his uncle's house along an ancient footpath which formerly ran through the yard of Shibden Hall. She also states that Sterne was a frequent visitor at Shibden Hall when her grandfather was a boy; and *he* was born in the same year as Sterne.

Is there however anything to confirm this? The Listers and Sternes were well acquainted, as Richard Sterne had married for his first wife the widow of Samuel Lister, by birth a Priestley. The Master of Hipperholme School was the Rev. Nathan Sharpe from 1703 to 1733; and he was connected with the Priestleys, for the Priestleys' arms were quartered with those of the Sharpes*. R. Sterne also speaks of his cousin Abraham Sharpe, who was appointed in 1727 to the Curacy of Sowerby Bridge; and one Abraham Sharpe of Hipperholme, Clerk, was married at Coley in 1727 to Ann Walker. R. Sterne, too, after his marriage, lived for six years at Shibden Hall. His daughter, Mary, is mentioned in P.R., under 1704, as being "baptised by Mr. Sharp", it being most unusual at that time to insert the name of the officiating clergyman: and it is somewhat singular that he should have been elected a Governor of Hipperholme

---

* Sharpe's arms are the same as those of the Sharpes of Horton, to which family Archbishop Sharpe belonged.

School in May, 1729. R. Sterne's family leanings then must have been towards Hipperholme School. Nathan Sharpe was in the prime of life in 1723, when Laurence was first "fixed at school", being then under fifty years of age, while Mr. Lister of Heath would be over sixty. I may add to this, that a Gentleman wrote to me from London in 1877, enquiring whether there were any registers belonging to the School, which contained the name of his Grandfather. He was in the habit, he said, of mentioning the anecdote of Laurence Sterne, as if the event which it records took place at the school, where he was educated about 1745. But the writer could not say whether he was at Heath or Hipperholme, and wished to know whether there was anything which would decide it.

It may be said, that Laurence was sent to Jesus College, because his master Mr. Lister was of that College; but, to say nothing of the fact that a goodly number from the West Riding happened to be members of that College about that time, Laurence's grandfather, the Archbishop, had been Master of the College, and had left money for four Scholarships in it; and one of the fellows, a Mr. Styan Thirlby, had got R. Sterne in 1729 to promise a subscription to a work in which he was interested, thus showing that there was still some sort of connection between the family and that College.

I must leave the matter unsettled. It is possible that Laurence was fixed at Heath and wrote his name there, but was afterwards removed to Hipperholme, when the infirmities of the Master at Heath caused the School to be neglected. The writing which was in existence in 1810 might have been a recent invention, a forgery in fact. The real writing must at that time have been faint, as 80 years had elapsed since Sterne's time: besides, the School-room had often been whitewashed, as the Governors allowed the Master annualy a guinea for that purpose.

Old Heath School — South View

Rath School
From a Drawing by W.H. Slifsord

CHAPTER XIV.

§1. THE OLD SCHOOL. §2. THE NEW SCHOOL.

§1. I HAVE said in Chap. V. §2 that we have no description of the School-buildings, except that Wright in 1738 spoke of a stately Grammar School whose building was fair, fine, and large. The Schools Inquiry Commission is content with saying that "the premises are old and have a reverend and quasi-ecclesiastical aspect". To help the memory of old pupils, I propose giving in this Chapter a brief description of the building with which they have so many associations. It was as they remember, obscured from the road by several insignificant and private buildings, and was approached through an uneven and almost private yard. One of the Lithographs in this work shews it as it would appear when divested of its external incumbrances. When examined carefully, it would seem as if it consisted of a long room with three Elizabethan Windows in the side, over which had been erected at a later period a series of dormitories, with four windows of a very cottage-like nature. It is probable that the school-room had originally a high-pitched roof, and it was found when the building was pulled down, that the old oak timbers had been used as far as they served, and the deficiencies were supplied by new deal. At the west end of the north side there was an entrance, screened from the north winds by a low porch. On entering, the pupil beheld a room which was fifty feet six inches long, twenty-one feet ten inches broad, and fourteen feet six inches high*. His eye would perhaps light first on the Master's awful desk at the east end, masking a door, by which he would afterwards frequently see a pleasant or frowning face emerge from the School-house : he would at first however become more familiar with the Usher's desk, which was placed near the entrance at the west end, exactly facing the Master's throne. As time went on, and he had opportunities of looking about him, he would observe three mullioned windows on the north side, each with two uprights and a transom, and three similiar windows on the south side, but each having *three* uprights and a transom. A few observant boys would discover that these windows were a foot broader than the northern ones†, and would account for it by the north side having to give room to a large fire-place as well as the entrance. But the most attractive sight to the new pupil would be a circular window‡ at the west end,

---

* This room ran so truly east and west that the rays of the setting sun on the day of the Autumnal Equinox shone straight through the west window. The house crossed the east end, due north and south, and projected beyond the school-room, so that the whole formed a Latin Cross with the eastern apex mutilated.

† I had several times set " The School-room " as a subject for a Theme, but I do not recollect any notice being taken of the difference of the windows, unless attention was previously called to it.

‡ This window was always very attractive : it is the only piece of the old building that now exists, and it is inserted in the north end of the drill shed, looking towards Free-school Lane. I have never seen any account of this window. According to the statements of persons connected with the New Buildings, it was an insertion in the old room after it had been completed, the stones round it not fitting in well, but having to be packed with clay and odd pieces of stone. There is a similar window over the porch of Elland New-hall, a building which was refronted by one of the Saviles about the same time as the School-room was built. Whether it was a design furnished by a local mason or copied from one at a distance, there is nothing to shew. In Dr. Favour's Subscription List, there is an item in Latin, of which the translation is " Will : Savile of Wakefield one glass window ", but there is nothing to prove its connection with the window in question, beyond the fact that a window was given by a Savile, and a window like ours was adopted in another Savile's residence about the same time. The only mention of our window that I have met with is in the Governors.' Account Book :—" 1775 Feb. 18 . Harper for Round Window £1. 1. 0 ". This would be for glazing, as the next account paid to Wm. & Jas. Harper is for ' new glazing '.

which he would soon learn to distinguish as the apple-and-
pear window, though he might at first imagine it to contain
a representation in glass of a series of sections of snail shells
revolving round a central circle. If he was inquisitive enough,
he might learn that it was a Catherine-wheel window, or
perhaps a rose window, or even be told that it was an oriel.
But it would ever be a puzzle, how or why it got there.
Some of his communicative school-fellows would soon be
asking him if he had ever heard of old Laury, and would
point out a partition of the ceiling where he was said to have
painted his name: and he would look at the 28 partitions
into which the ceiling was divided by the beams that supported
the dormitories, and wonder if he could not himself do something of the kind in future days; but he would soon find an
easier way of transmitting his name to after days as he looked
at the wainscoting that surrounded the room, ancient and
venerable in his eyes, but in reality of so late a date as 1816.
If his position allowed him, his eyes would often be taken
from his book, by the Stancliffe Tablet on the north side, and
he would gaze and gaze again at the awful head on its top,
which he would irreverently style "the Nigger", though
he might be emboldened some day with school-boy wit to
put a pipe in its mouth. And if transferred, as he might
be, to the opposite side of the room, he might (if he was a
pupil in the last days) have gazed wistfully at the Tablet
which told the Scholarships and the Honour of Senior Classic
gained by a former pupil, J. W. Bonser, between 1866 and
1870, dreaming perhaps that such things were often done,
but not knowing that few schools except the greatest ever
gain such a distinction as Senior Classic. There would be
nothing else to engage his attention: he would not care to
know that the sash windows* went out, and diamond panes

---

* There might have been some names of interest scratched on these, but none
attracted my attention, as I had then but recently come to Halifax, except
"John Lonsdale 1706".

came in, with the New Year 1862, and that the desk at which he sat, consisting of a sloping slab of wood on an iron frame that was screwed down to the floor, was no older than the diamond panes. Often however did he feel annoyed by the stone floor on which he had to stand, though there was wood where he sat, and at the distance which lay between him and the fire, a distance so severely felt on a cold day, especially if he was in one of the upper classes.

§2. *(Contributed by the Architects themselves.)* The New School Buildings are adjacent to the site of the old School and are designed in the Elizabethan style of Architecture, a feeling having been expressed by some of the Governors for the style of Architecture prevalent in the district at the time the old Building was erected. It having been thought judicious that some relic of the Old School should be perpetuated, the " Apple and Pear " window is placed in the North Gable of the Covered Drill Shed, and a replica of the same window introduced into the Centre Gable of the New Building.

The Plan of the School Building is somewhat in the form of the letter E, the long side of which is towards Free School Lane, and set back 50 feet from the road. The Centre Arm is formed by the Assembly Hall, which is placed longitudinally.

Referring to the Ground Floor, a corridor eight feet wide runs the whole length of the Building, and from it, to the right of the entrance Hall, access is obtained to the following rooms :—Cloak Room, with ingress and egress doors, Lavatory, Library 18 feet by 12 feet 6 inches, and two Class Rooms, each 20 feet by 18 feet. To the left of the Hall there are four rooms, one being the Masters' Room 18 feet by 14 feet, and the other Class Rooms each 20 feet by 18 feet. Opening out of the Vestibule is the Porter's Room, while directly opposite the entrance is the Assembly Room 50 feet by 30 feet. This, the principal department in the Building, has a Queen Post open timbered roof ornamented with the character-istics of the style. In addition to the Main Entrance doors this room has two side doors for the use of the Masters.

The first floor is reached from the entrance Hall by an open stone staircase, with oak balustrade, newels, etc., and together with the Vestibule doors, arching, etc., forms a characteristic feature of the interior of the Building. The main staircase is lighted from the recessed portion shewn in the front view, which, while fully answering the desired end, assists in breaking up what would otherwise be a long and perhaps monotonous frontage.

The rooms on the first floor are disposed somewhat similarly to those on the ground floor, and comprise a Museum 28 feet by 18 feet, Science Room 27 feet by 20 feet, Laboratory 20 feet by 18 feet, and private Laboratory (for the use of the instructor in science) 18 feet by 12 feet. These Rooms are en suite. To the left of the Staircase there is a Class Room 20 feet by 18 feet, then the School of Art Department consisting of three Rooms somewhat similar to the Science Rooms.

In the sub-ground floor is located the Dining Room 35 feet by 18 feet, easily accessible from the entrance Hall. A Cooking Kitchen, China Closet, Lavatory, etc., are connected with the Dining Room, while to the back are situated the apartments of the caretaker.

To the south-west of the School Building are situated the Covered Drill Ground (50 feet by 33 feet) and the Gymnasium (50 feet by 24 feet), the latter having attached to it two small rooms, also a Gallery for visitors with access from the covered Drill Ground.

The warming and ventilation to the School Building are upon the most approved methods. The rooms, etc., have rows of hot water pipes upon the low pressure system which

is considered the most healthful. The Masters' Room and
Dining Room have fireplaces in them, in addition to being
warmed by hot water pipes. The Ventilation is effected by
Boyle's patent outlets, and Shillito & Shoreland's patent
Vertical pipe inlets.

The work has been executed by the following Contractors
who are all local men:—Masonry by Messrs. Chas. Bolton
& Co.; Joinery, by Messrs. S. Wadsworth & Son; Slating
and Plastering, by Mr. Alf. S. Blackburn; Plumbing, Glazing,
and Heating Apparatus, by Mr. John Naylor; Painting,
Mr. Jonas Binns; Iron Railing and Gates, by Messrs. Hirst
Bros.; the Locks and Ironmongery were supplied by Mr.
R. W. Parkin, of Sowerby Bridge.

The Architects are Messrs. Leeming & Leeming, of
Northgate Chambers, Halifax, and Mr. R. J. Bryan has
acted as Clerk of the Works.

Operations were commenced by the Contractors in August
1877. The Old School was vacated in April 1879, and with
many inconveniences the New Buildings were first used on
April 17th, but as new furniture was required, and the
approaches and play-ground were unfinished, there was no
formal opening. The old buildings have been removed, and
some alterations in the Master's house are still in progress
(October, 1879), but some time will yet elapse before all is
complete. But when finished, the building, with school
furniture of the newest design, will be well worthy of
inspection; and then, "Open, Sesame!"

CHAPTER XV.

§1. THE EARLY GOVERNORS.   §2. THE GOVERNORS UNDER THE
CHARTER OF 1729.   §3. LIST OF GOVERNORS FROM
1584 TO 1875.   §4. THE GOVERNING BODY
UNDER THE NEW SCHEME.

§1. WE have three lists of the first Governors of the
School; one in the Charter itself, another (in the
Parish Registers) with their residences annexed, and a third
in Brearcliffe's MS. together with their successors. There
is also in P.R. a list of those who were elected on the death
of the first "before the School was built" in 1598.   It is
difficult to make out the exact succession; even Brearcliffe
differs from the P.R., and we have no record at all of the
election of some.   The date on the left of the names in the
accompanying Table is that of election, except when in a
parenthesis; then, it denotes merely some year in which their
names happen to be mentioned: the date on the right is that
of death or resignation.   The line just before 1607 shews that
there was a break in the line of succession.   There is also
no account of Governors in the latter part of the seventeenth
century and the beginning of the eighteenth.

As the first Governors belonged to the most important
families of the neighbourhood, some notice of them may be
interesting, as the families to which they belonged have
altogether passed away.

(1.) John Lacy was the eldest son of Hugh Lacy of
Cromwell-bottom, and belonged to a family which once
possessed the largest estates in the West Riding.   He lived
at Brearley in Midgley, not far from Mytholmroyd.   His
mother was a Savile, one of his sisters married John Deane,

another Governor, and Vicar Ashburne married Elizabeth
Lacy, probably another sister. He died in 1585, shortly
after the Charter of the School was signed. His son John
was elected Governor in his place: he sold Brearley. The
Ashburnes were on very good terms with the Lacys, as one
of them lent the little bell of the Parish Church to Brearley,
where there was probably a private chapel, which was not
returned until the latter end of 1626, when it was "fetched
back again", as the Register says.

(2.) John Savile was the eldest son of Henry Savile, of
Bradley in Stainland, and Ellen Ramsden. He was born
in 1545, and sent to Brasenose College, Oxford, in 1561.
He left it without taking a Degree, going to the Inner Temple
in London to study the Law. He became Sergeant of Law
in 1594, was made a member of the Council of the North,
which had its Head quarters at York, and was appointed
Baron of the Exchequer in 1598. Though interested more
than others in the foundation of our School, he was taken
away from the neighbourhood so much by his public duties,
without having any one to feel the interest in the School
which he himself felt, that his laudable desires were on the
point of failure; and all the efforts made and the expense
incurred would have been in vain, had it not been for the
zealous co-operation of Dr. Favour, in whom he seems to
have placed the greatest confidence. He had collected
together a most influential body of Governors, his neighbours
and friends, but, for some cause or other, they were incapable
of joint action.

(3.) Brian Thornhill lived at Fixby Hall, which his
ancestors had occupied for 200 years. His grandmother was
Janet Savile of Newhall. He belonged to a younger branch
of the family, the eldest having ended in Elizabeth Thornhill,
who married Henry Savile and lived at Thornhill, near

Wakefield. Brian died without issue, and his brother John succeeded him in the estates, and was elected a Governor on his death.

(4.) Francis Ashburne became Vicar of Halifax on the resignation of his father in 1573. He married Elizabeth Lacy, and died in 1585.

(5.) Henry Savile lived at Blaidroyd in Southowram, sometimes called 'The Bank'. His mother was a Savile, of Copley, and his great-grandmother a Lacy. He afterwards came to live at Shaw-hill, and died in London in 1617.

(6.) Henry Farrar lived at Ewood, not far from Brearley in Midgley, a manor which came to him on his marriage with Mary, the daughter of John Lacy. He paid the expense incurred in obtaining the Charter of the School.

(7.) William Dean of Exley married into the family of John Hanson, who was another Governor, and was connected also with the Wades. His brother's grand-daughter was the wife of the celebrated Bishop Lake. The estate of Exley was subsequently sold to the Greames.

(8.) Robert Wade lived at Fieldhouse in Sowerby, which he had bought of Henry Farrar. His family became connected by marriage with the Hansons, the Deanes, and the Ramsdens.

(9.) John Deane was of Deane-house in Midgley, and so was close neighbour to the Lacys and the Farrars. His wife was a sister of John Lacy. He had "departed with his family out of the Vicarage and Parish of Halifax" before January 1607, as the Parish Register tell us.

(10.) Anthony Hyrst or Hurst belonged to Greetland. I have found nothing whatever about him, except that his son Henry was Governor in his stead before 1598.

(11.) George Firthe lived at Firthhouse, which was at the extremity of Barkisland most remote from Halifax. His house subsequently came by purchase into the possession of the Hortons, who pulled it down and built a new house on the site. He is mentioned in a will in 1588 with George and John Savile.

(12.) John Hanson of Woodhouse, Junior. He lived at Woodhouse in Rastrick. His family was connected with the Saviles by marriage, and also with the Wades. Some of the Hansons were the great lawyers of the neighbourhood, and great antiquarians. Nicholas, the brother of John, describes himself in his will as "one of the servants and clerks of Sir John Savile".

The brief account which I have given of the original Governors will serve to shew that they were very closely connected together by marriage or neighbourhood. They lived for the most part at a distance from the town of Halifax, and grouped themselves round the Saviles at Bradley, or the Lacys at Brearley, and so represented the Parish rather than the Town of Halifax; and, as I said before, the School was accidentally situated near the Town, because the Saviles and Farrars had some waste land that they could afford to part with in the neighbourhood.

The twelve Governors, whom I have mentioned, are specified by name in the Original Charter. It is also there stated that "there shall be for ever within the said Parish "and Vicarage of Halifax twelve of the discreetest and "honestest men dwelling within the same Parish and Vicarage "for the time being which shall be called the Governors of "the possessions revenues and goods of the Free Grammar "School .... during their lives so that they use themselves "well and faithfully towards the said School .... Whensoever "any one or more die or otherwise dwell out of the said "Parish and Vicarage of Halifax and with their family depart "thence the other Governors .... [shall] choose and nominate "any other meet person or persons .... being above the "age of twenty-four years &c." The election wss to be made within a month of the vacancy, and if "it was not made in form", the Archbishop of York was to elect. The Governor elect was to take an oath, and could not act until he had done so.

N.B.—There was no ex-officio Governor, as used to be supposed. No Vicar of Halifax seems to have been Governor between 1712 and 1779.

§2. I have in Chap. VII. given an account of the confirmation of the Charter in 1729. There is very little necessity for going into detail respecting the new Governors. The reader will remember Mr. Lister's letter, in which their nomination is atttributed solely to Mr. Sterne. But he seems to have had some difficulty· in getting a suitable body to act with him. Mr. Lister·speaks of himself as having been applied to, and also of a Mr. Turner (about whom I find no further mention); he puts in his list a Mr. Ramsbothom also, and leaves out the old Governor, Mr. Greame, as if he had been at first unwilling to continue in office, though Mr. Sterne had two months before sent only eleven names to the Archbishop. He was probably gained over by Mr. Sterne, as no one would have been left to administer the oath of qualification. At any rate Mr. Lister's letter shews that there were doubts even after Mr. Sterne's nomination of eleven. Many hung back, having taken fright probably at the pecuniary difficulties which Trustees had recently encountered. The nucleus of the new body was Mr. Sterne; he first gained over his father-in-law, Mr. Booth; there would not be much difficulty in persuading John and James Batley, Mr. Farrar, and Mr. Ramsbothom, who had suffered directly or indirectly from the decision of the Commission, mentioned in Chap. VII. Mr. Burton's name was perhaps added out of compliment. I do not find any mention of

the four others. He would probably have a difficulty on
Mr. Ramsbothom's refusal to serve, as he certainly had when
Mr. Burton, Mr. Stot, and Mr. Ramsden declined: but he
eventually got over all obstacles, and was able to fill up the
vacancies. One of the three Governors elected after the
receipt of the Charter, W. Walker, was perhaps a relation
of R. Walker, whose estate had felt the Commission's heavy
hand. Mr. Sterne's success did good service to the School,
though his plan had had its origin in a discreditable state
of things, to say the least. He had evidently to pay for it;
but it was to his special perseverance that the School at
length became useful to the community, and was more closely
connected with the Town and its immediate neighbourhood.
From his time there has never been wanting a succession
of faithful and conscientious Governors, to whose able discharge
of their duties special testimony was borne in the Report
of the Schools Inquiry Commission. Thus was good evolved
out of evil, and selfishness used as an instrument to promote
the general welfare.

§3. LIST OF GOVERNORS FROM 1584 TO 1875.

1.			2.		
1584	John Lacy	Aug. 1585	1584	John Savile	Feb. 1604
	John Lacy (son)				
1607	Anthony Wade	1620	1607	Henry Savile (son)	Sep. 1632
	Jo: Fourness				
(1624)	Richard Dearden	Jun. 1626			
(1629)	Thomas Whitley				
(1635)	John Whitley		(1635)	John Savile	
(1714)	Henry Greame	1739 Nov.			
(1727)	,,		1727	Richard Sterne	Oct. 1732
(1744)	Christopher Rawson		1762	John Ramsden (of Well-head)	(resd.)
			1788	William Grimshaw	
1780	John Rawson (of Stoney Royd)	1815	1795	Josh. Priestley	1819
1816	John Rawson (of the Shay)		1828	George Priestley	(resd.)
1820	William John Norris		1838	John Rawson	
1837	Charles Norris		1854	William Henry Rawson	
1838	John Rawson (of Brockwell)				

LIST OF GOVERNORS FROM 1584 TO 1875.

3.			4.		
1584	Brian Thornhill	Oct. 1598	1584	Francis Ashburne	Jul. 1585
	John Thornhill (brother)			Henry Ledsham	(resd.) 1593
	John Thornhill (son)			John Favour	Mar. 162$\frac{3}{4}$
1612	Thomas Thornhill (brother)		1624	Robert Clay	Apr. 1828
				Hugh Ramsden	Jul. 1629
				Henry Ramsden	Mar. 163$\frac{5}{6}$
				Richard Marsh	(resd.) 1662
1727	Timothy Booth	Dec. 1736	1727	Thomas Burton	(declined)
			1729(?)	James Tetlay (Tetlow)	
(1744)	Samuel Lister		1753	Cyril Jackson	⎫
1766	William Haigh		,,	Luke Hoyle	⎬ (declined)
1778	Thomas Dyson		,,	Rev. John Lister	⎭
1790	Samuel Lees		1754	Valentine Stead	
1808	George Greenup		1761	Joseph Bramley	
1837	Mason Stanhope Kenny (resd.)		1787	John Bramley	
1863	Thomas William Rawson		1812	Stansfeld Rawson	(resd.)
1864	John Edward Wainhouse (resd.)		1827	George Pollard	May 1866
1871	Thomas Turlay	Sep. 1871	1866	John Staveley	Jan. 1870
			1870	Joshua Appleyard	

LIST OF GOVERNORS FROM 1584 TO 1875.

5.		6.	
1584	Henry Savile	1584	Henry Farrar
1607			
	Anthony Foxcroft	1611	John Brigge	Feb. 1613
		1613	William Harrison	Jul. 1618
		(1629)	Humphres Drake	
		(1634)	John Drake	Jun. 1642
1727	James Batley	1727	Robert Ramsden	Aug. 1750
			(of Siddal Hall)	
1749	James Wetherherd	1750	John Waterhouse	
1778	William Newby	1759	Samuel Lees	
1801	William Rawson	1761	Luke Hoyle	
1828	Edward Wainhouse (resd.)	1770	George Smith	
1837	John Staveley (resd.)	1778	Thomas Preston	Nov. 1821
1854	Edward Akroyd	1822	Thomas Preston (Junr.)	
		1837	Edward Rawson	

124

LIST OF GOVERNORS FROM 1584 TO 1875.

7.		8.	
1584	William Deane	1584 Robert Wade	Dec. 1594
	Robert Deane *(son)*	Gilbert Saltenstall	Dec. 1598
		Richard Sunderland	Jun. 1634
		(1635) Abraham Sunderland	1643
1727	Henry Haigh	1727 Elkanah Farrar	
1752	John Baldwin	1760 William Greame	
1779	Henry Wood *(Vicar)* Oct. 1790	1766 John Edwards	
1790	Henry Wm.CoulthurstDec.1817	(1792) John Edwards	(resd.)
1818	Samuel Knight Jan. 1827	1814 Henry Lees Edwards	
1827	Charles Musgrave Apr. 1875	1848 Henry Edwards	

LIST OF GOVERNORS FROM 1584 TO 1875.

9.

1584	John Deane	(resd.) (?)

1607 Isaak Waterhouse Feb. 160₁⁰₀
Anthony Waterhouse Mar. 162¾
John Clough

1727 John Stot (declined)
(1745) W. Walker
1787 William Smith
1798 John Priestley
1801 Josh. Lister
1818 John Dearden
1838 John Dearden (Junr.)
1839 John Edwards Dyson
1840 William Haigh
1854 George Haigh (resd.)
1862 William Rothwell

10.

1584 Anthony Hyrst
Henry Hyrst (son)

(1624) John Cooper
(1635) James Murgatroyd

1727 John Batley
1760 John Waterhouse
1802 John Waterhouse
1848 John Waterhouse 1879

11.	12.
1584 George Firth	1584 John Hanson 1621
(1611) Robert Hemingway Mar. 161¾	John Thorp
(1624) Jasper Blythman	(1627) Nathaniel Waterhouse Jun.1645
(1629) Samuel Lister	
Thomas Lister Jan. 167⅞	
1727 Robert Ramsden (declined) (*of Wharlehouse*)	1727 Richard Taylor
(1744) John Lodge	1763 Thomas Ramsden
1768 John Winn (declined)	1787 Robert Parker
,, John Royds	1796 Charles Hudson
1781 Richard Royds	1815 John Dyson (*of Willow Field*)
1806 John Haigh	1818 Robert Paley, M.D. (resd.)
1826 Thomas Ramsden (*of Heath Hall*)	1828 Jeremiah Rawson
1852 Thomas Robson Feb. 1877	1839 Samuel Waterhouse
	1852 Samuel Waterhouse (Junr.)

§4. THE GOVERNING BODY UNDER THE NEW SCHEME.

Some of the regulations made by the Endowed Schools
Commission concerning the Governors are stated in their
Scheme as follows:—

"The Governing Body shall ultimately consist of fifteen
persons, of whom two shall be *ex officio* Governors, nine
representative or elective, and four co-optative.

"The *ex officio* Governors shall be The Mayor of Halifax,
and The Chairman of the School Board of Halifax, if they
will respectively undertake to act.

"The Representative Governors shall be elected, Four
by the Municipal Corporation of Halifax; Two by the School
Board of Halifax; One by the Governing Body of the
Hipperholme Grammar School; One by the Governing Bodies
of the Endowed School at Boothtown, founded by Jeremiah
Hall, and of the Endowed School at Elland, founded by Joseph
Brooksbank, alternately; One by the Governing Bodies of
the Endowed School at Rastrick, founded by Mary Law,
and of the Endowed School at Sowerby, founded by Paul
Bairstow, alternately.

"The Representative Governors shall be elected to office
for the term of five years, and at the expiry of such term
shall be re-eligible.

"The Co-optative Governors shall be appointed to the office
for the term of eight years, and be capable of re-appointment.
The first Co-optative Governors (1873) shall be appointed to
office for life, being the eleven present Governors.

"Women may be Governors.

The first Members of the new Governing Body were:—

EX-OFFICIO. {	Thomas Wayman	*Mayor.*
	John Henry Swallow	*Chairman of School Board.*
REPRESENTATIVE. {	John Dyson Hutchinson*	}
	Samuel Thomas Midgley	
	John William Longbottom	} *Elected by the Town Council,* 1874.
	Nathan Whitley	
	James Hope †	} *Elected by the School Board,* 1874.
	John Edwards Hill	
‡		
CO-OPTATIVE. {	Charles Musgrave	(*died* 1875.)
	John Waterhouse	(*died* 1879.)
	Edward Rawson	
	Henry Edwards	
	Thomas Robson	(*died* 1877.)
	Samuel Waterhouse	
	William Henry Rawson	
	Edward Akroyd	
	William Rothwell	
	Joshua Appleyard	
	John Rawson	

* Oct., 1879, Mr. Alderman Hutchinson not seeking re-election, Mr. Councillor Hall was chosen in his stead ; the other Members of the Council were re-elected.

† Oct., 1879, The Rev. James Hope being no longer a member of the School Board, Mr. Alfred Ramsden was elected in his stead. Mr. Hill was re-elected.

‡ Mrs. Judd was subsequently elected as representative of the Endowed School at Rastrick.

N.B.—Mr. Edward Crossley also acted as Governor, during his Mayoralty, from November 1874 to November 1876.

CHAPTER XVI.

A COPY of the Deed by which the Saviles conveyed their gift of land is in the Parish Register. As it is not only in Latin, but also has many contractions, I will present it to the reader in an English dress.

Let present and future know that we the Honourable Lord Gilbert Earl of Shrewsbury of the noble Order of the Garter Knight, Edward Saville Esquire son and heir of Henry Savile Knight deceased lately Lord of the Manor of Skircot in the county of York and George Savile Knight, have enfeoffed delivered granted and of love towards our country and good learning have confirmed to the Governors of the possessions revenues and goods of the Free Grammar School of Queen Elizabeth in the parish of Halifax in the county of York commonly named "The Free Grämer schole of Queen Elizabeth" by virtue of a royal licence under the great seal of England bearing date at Westminster the fifteenth day of February in the twenty-seventh year of the reign of the said Lady the Queen one messuage or house called " a Schole-howse" lately built and six acres of land, weak stony and bruery [debilis lapidosæ et bruer'] by estimation now [modo] of the annual value of eight pence lying contiguous, about the said messuage with the pertinences [cum p'tinen'] in Skircot aforesaid lying and existing on the south side of the messuage and land in the same place now [modo] in the tenure of Michael Smyth and abutting on the land of the same Michael on the north side, on the waste or common of Skircot on the west and south sides and on the same common and the land of Abraham Milner on the east side. To have and to hold the aforesaid messuage or house called "a Schole-howse" and the aforesaid six acres of land weak, stony and bruery with the aforesaid pertinences to the forementioned governors and their successors, to hold of the chief lords of that fee by the services thence due and of right accustomed. And we indeed the forementioned Earl Edward Savile, and George Savile Knight and our heirs the aforesaid messuage or house called "a Schole-howse" and the aforesaid six acres of land weak, stony and bruery with the pertinences to the forementioned Governors and their Successors against us and our heirs will guarantee and for ever defend by [these] presents. . . .

In testimony of which we have put to this present document of ours our seals. Dated the fourteenth day of August in the fortieth year of the reign of our aforesaid Lady Elizabeth by the grace of God Queen of England France and Ireland defender of the faith, in the year of the Lord 1598.

Gilb: Shrewsbery. Edward Savill: George Savill. Sealed and delivered on the 4th day of October in the year below written at "Sheffield Lodge*", with the grant of the below written George Savill Knight of four oaks in "Eland p'ke" [park] for building the School below specified. George Savile. Jo: Savile. Jo: Lacy. Hen: Savile, Randale Catherall, nicol. Hanson. 1598.

---

* Sheffield Lodge or Manor was built as a country-house in Sheffield Park some two miles from Sheffield about the beginning of the sixteenth century by George, the fourth Earl. Hunter in his "Hallamshire" gives a view of what was left when he wrote his work.

I propose now to lay before my readers some of the early Subscription-lists which are to be found in the Parish Registers. Brearcliffe has them also in his MSS., though occasionally a difference occurs. On consideration I give them in their original Latin, because misinterpretations have been given of them or false deductions drawn from them, and will append a few notes.

I.

Nomina benefactorū p' edificatione scholæ de Halifax, habitātiū ext. p'och de Hal.

1. Rich. Saltēstall miles Maior Londō   iii[lb] 6[s] 8[d]
2. Gibt[s] comes Salop: et eius comitissa impetratu
   Geor. Savile dono dederūt   4[or] querc'
3. Henric[s] Savile p'pos: collegij Eton et cust[s]
   colleg. Mertonēsis in Oxon. [Provost of Eton College and Warden of Merton College in Oxford] xl[s]
4. Will. Thornhill canonics[s] Wigor. [Canon of Worcestor] xl[s]
5. Robt[s] Kaye de Woodsame armig.   xx[s]
6. Guil. Ramsden de Longley armig.   xx[s]
7. Jo: Jackson de Etherthorpe armig.   xx[s]
8. Edw. Mawde vic' de Wakfeelde   x[s]
9.   Bilsbye ostiari[s] scaccarij [Usher of the Exchequer] x[s]
10. Tho. Crosland de Northcrosland   x[s]
11. Nicol. Feney, quōd. schol.   Hal.   x[s]
12. Tho. Norcliffe nat[s] in Barksland   x[s]
13.+Jo: Nalson de Mcathley in Lyme   xii[s]+
14. Michael Doughty gen: nat[s] in Ovēd   xl[s]
15. David Wat'house cle. coronæ bāc: reg.*   xl[s]
16. Jo: Milner gen. quōd schol: Hal   x[s]
17. Jo: Preestley ar. nat[s] in Soarby   x[s]

* "Clerk of the Crown of the Queen's Bench".

18. Jacob^s Stansfeeld armig.   x^s
19. Tho: Pilkington armig.   xx^s
20. Will. Ashton de Clegg   `x^s
21. Rich. Cole armig   x^s
22. Jo: Lister Aldermānus de Hull   iij^{lb}
23. Jaspar Blythman armig.   xl^s
24. Edw. Ashton Rector de Middletō   xx^s
25.   Shuttleworth et Jo: Preestley sup^a noīat^s ⎫
       executores   Michel* Rect: de Oxhill in ⎬ iiij^{lb}
       comit. Warw.   ⎭
26. Guil. Savile de Wakfeeld vitri. unā fenestr
27. Rich: Bewmont de Wh. armig.   xx^s
28. Jo: Ramsden Gen.   xx^s
29. Samuel Saltēstall de Hūswick gē.   xx^s
30. Robt^s Waterhouse de Harthill   x^s
31. Josuah Smith vic' hudd'feld   x^s
32. Jo: Armitage ar.   x^s
33. Robt^s Nettleton de Almōbery   x^s
34. Edward^s Copley de Batley, arm: xx^s
35. Alexand^r Stocke Rector de Heaton.   xx^s
36.†A Doct. Benet Cancel. Eborac' p' p'te pænit: ⎫
       xpoph^r Oldfeeld adulterij crimine cōvicti. ⎭ xl^s
37. Henry Foxcroft de Batley gen.   x^s
38. Marmaduke Eland gen.   x^s

                               Sū   xl^{lb.}   vj^s   8d‡

---

* Henry Michell was Rector of Oxhill near Kineton in South Warwickshire
from 20 Jan., 1558, to 1597. It is worth noting that from this Church (a
remarkable Norman building) the clerk followed by the congregation turned out
on Sunday, Oct. 23rd, 1642, to witness the battle at Edgehill. I think that the
Rector belonged to the Mitchells of Scowt in Shibden.

† It is singular that Doctor Benet L.L.D. was in 1616 Chancellor of Canterbury,
when the will of Gilbert Earl of Shrewsbury, mentioned at the beginning of this
List, was proved before him.

‡ In this sum the writer has left out the value of the lime 12s., which will
account for +..+ in that item. B. has also read + as if it were 4, and so made
£40 19 0.

II.

Nõia benefactorū in p'ochia de Halifax inhabitātiū p'
edificat: scholæ et īmuratione eiusdē et terrarū eidem
contigue adiacētiū

39. Henric[s] Farrar Ar. chartā incorporationis suis sūptib[s] et
labore procuravit et obtinuit.

40. Joan. Savile serviens ad legē *(serjeant at law)*	v [℔]
41. Bria: Thornhill cū Jo: fratre	6 querc[s]
42. Joan. Favour ll. Doctor in pecū: Dictio: Anglicolat: Lexi. græcolat	
43. Joan. Lacy de Briarley ar.	4 querc[s]
44. Jacob: Kinge de Sk. testa*: leg:	v [℔] -
45. Tho: Hopkinson de Eland test: leg:	x[s]
46. Jo: Hanson Senior de Woodhouse	xxv[s]
47. Jo: Longbothā de North. test: leg:	v [℔]
48. Rich: Townend p' testam.	iij[℔] vj[s] 8[d]
49. Antony Hurst de greetl. p' test.	xl[s]
50. Tho: Haworth de Hal p' test.	xx[s]
Halifax	
Daniel Foxcrofte	xl[s] et xx[s]
Robt Greenefeeld	xl[s] et xx[s]
Robt Lawe	xl[s]
Brian Crowther	xl[s]
Edward Broadley	xl[s]
John Waterhouse	xxx[s]
Willm Harison	xxx[s]
Vid. Will. Baerstow (*Vid.* is *Widow*)	xx[s]
Rich. Lawe	xx[s]
Joa: Baerstowe cū ux. fil. *(i.e. with his wife's son)*	xxx[s]
Tho: Warde	xx[s]

---

* test., testa:, testam:, mean *will,* and leg: *legavit* or *bequeathed:* p' is for
per i.e. by.

Robt. Greenwoode	xx^s
Robt Exley	xx^s
Henry Hoyle	xx^s
John Mawde	xx^s
Rich. Maye	xx^s
Josephe Wormale	$xiij^s\ 4^d$
John Wilson	$xiij^s\ 4^d$
	$xxv^{lb}\ xvi^s\ viii^d$
a reliquis inhabitãtib^s ⎱ in minorib^s sūmis ⎰	$xv^{lb}\ i^s\ ix^d$
Sū	$40^{lb}\ xviij^s\ v^d$

Skircote

Isaake Waterhouse de Woodhouse	$iij^{lb}\ 6^s\ 8^d$
Anton. Wade de Kingcross	$iij^{lb}\ vi^s\ 8^d$
Jacob: Kinge sup^a noīat^s	xl^s
Rich: Waterhouse Mertleb. (?)	xx^s
Edward Whitakers cũ fil. Edw	$xxvi^s\ 8^d$
John Lockwood	xx^s
a reliquis	$ij^{lb}\ xiiij^s\ iiij^d$
Sū	14 ·· 14 ·· 4

It would be too tedious to put down all the minor sums added to the Subscription from the various Townships: it will be sufficient to give the sum total collected in each.

	£	s.	d.		£	s.	d.
Sowerby	13	4	2	Stainland	1	11	6
Warley ...	7	14	8	Rastrick-cum-			
Ovenden	6	7	0	Toothill	1	2	10
Northowram ...	10	18	10	Fixby	0	14	6
Hipperholme ...	6	9	6	Heptonstall... ...	2	0	2
Southowram ...	8	1	2	Stansfeild ...	2	2	6
Midgley	3	16	4	Waddesworth	3	4	8
Shelf	1	10	0	Eringden ...	0	18	2
Elland-cum-				Langfeild	0	17	6
Greetland ...	5	9	4	John Hogg of Shelf	5	13	4
Barkisland	1	16	8	*(by will)*			
Rishworth-cum-				John Northend of			
Norland ...	2	9	1	Folde in North-owram	1	0	0
				(by will)			
	£67	16	9		19	5	2
					67	16	9
					£87	1	11

SUMMARY.

				£	s.	d.
I. Subscriptions outside the Parish	...	40	6	8
II.(a)	„	in the Parish	... ...	23	1	8
(b)	„	in Halifax	25	16	8
(c)	„	„ (in small sums)...	15	1	9
(d)	„	in Skircote	14	14	4
(e)	„	in other Townships	87	1	11
			£206	3	0

I think that anyone will be able to make out the above list, if he knows that 'comes' means *Earl*, 'miles' *knight*, ar. arm. armig. *esquire*, and gen. (for generosus) *gentleman*. He must also know that (–) over a letter denotes the omission of *m* or *n*, and that *s* at the end of the word is for *us*, and that Sū is for *Summa, i.e, Sum Total*. The heading of the first list is, in English, "Names of the benefactors for *(pro)* the building of the School of Halifax, dwelling outside the parish of Halifax", and that of the second is "Names of benefactors dwelling in the parish of Halifax for the building of the School and the walling of the same and of the lands contiguously adjacent to the same". I have found out a great deal of information with respect to all the subscribers except Bilsbye, Crosland, Cole, and Lockwood; but it would only encumber this work to give it. If any one will look at a Map of the West Riding, he will see that most of the subscribers lived in the country extending between Stainland and Wakefield, a country in which the Savile influence was very great at the time. It is necessary to state what is meant by some places. Etherthorpe or Edderthorpe, *i. e.*, Edric-thorpe, was in Darfield, and was held by a son-in-law of Sir J. Savile; Huntswick or Huntwick was between Wakefield and Pontefract; Clegg was in Rochdale parish, but the Ashtons both of that and of Middleton were connected with the West Riding families; Harthill was near Sheffield, but its owner was connected with the Waterhouses of Shibden; and Eland (38) lived at Carlinghow near Batley. There is a difficulty in one or two points. I do not know why Feney (11) and Milner (16) are spoken of as *quondam schol.* (scholars?), as the School was not yet built. A Nicholas Feney died in Almondbury in 1616, aged 78, and it is said that the family then became extinct. Bilsbye, Cole, and Benet (who was LL.D. and a civilian) were probably connected with the courts, which Sir John Savile had to do with, either at York or Westminster: It is singular that the will of the Earl of Shrewsbury, who is at the head of the List, was proved in 1616 before Dr. Benet, whose name is at the end. There is something curious about (13). There were Nalsons* at Methley in Henry the Eighth's reign, but it was a pretty good distance for twelve shillings-worth of lime to travel. This is the only instance of an English Word in the lists, which are in Latin, and also of the value of material being given. But it was evidently an after-thought, for it is not reckoned in the sum total.

Almost every one in the Halifax List bore office, either as Churchwarden or Constable, and so came under the influence of Dr. Favour. Edward Whitakers was Rector of Thornhill, and therefore a dependent of the Saviles. It seems clear then that Sir John Savile, or his agent Dr. Favour, got most of the subscriptions. But the principal ones were got outside the parish, and very little credit is due to what we now call the Town of Halifax, except as regards Brian Crowther's Legacy.

As regards (42), we may say that what Dr. Favour gave in money he kept secret to himself; but it was well known that the School owed to him a Latin-English Dictionary and a Greek-Latin Lexicon, and also a large Bible. (See p. 19.) He also mentions in one of his letters (L.P.CL.) that he and Sir John Savile had been "enforced to enlarge their benevolence above that that they had before given". The lists in P.R. were probably drawn up after his death.

---

* In 1635 a "Mr. Nelson" of *Hipperholme* subscribes 10s. 0d. There were Nelsons or Nalsons in possession of Dove House near there. I have thought it possible that 'in Lyme' may be some corruption of Mytholme written badly, just as Mertlob: is of Mear Clough Bottom.

We also find the following in the Parish Register : —
December 3 Anno Dni 1635.

A particular of such moneyes as have been given towards
the purchase of lands for the free grammar schoole of Queene
Elizabeth neare Hallifax this last yeare and collected by
Henry Ramsden vicar of Hallifax. The summe to be collected
was one hundred four score and tenne pounds.

Given by such as live out of the Vicaredge.

Imprimis (55) Mr.Charles Greenwood parson of Thornhill £20 0 0

Itm (56) Mr. Beniamen Wade of New Grange   5 0 0

Itm (57) Mr. Okewell vicar of Bradford   5 0 0

Itm (58) Mr. Nicoll minister of Thorneton   1 0 0

Given by the governors of the said schoole

Imprimis (59) Mr. John Savile of Methley, esquier   5 0 0

Item out of moneyes left by (60) Mr. Richard
Sunderland of Coley Hall Esquier deceased to } 10 0 0
be disposed of by his sons to good uses

Itm (61) Mr. Abraham Sunderland esquier   6 0 0

Itm (62) Mr. John ffarrer esquier   3 6 8

Itm (63) Mr. James Murgetroid   5 0 0

Itm (64) Mr. Daniell ffoxcroft   5 0 0

Itm (65) Mr. John Drake, Horley Green   5 0 0

Itm (66) Mr. John Whitley of Wheatley   2 0 0

    72 6 8

Summary of small Subscriptions.

Halifax	...	... £41	5	8	Sowerby	... ... £10	2	8
Northowram		14 16	4		Warley	... 7	5	0
Southowram	...	17 16	8		Hipperholme	6	3	4
Midgley		1 13	4		Shelf...	3	0	0
Skircoat	... ...	5 11	8		Norland	4	10	0
Ovenden	... ...	10 1	8		Rushworth	... 0	5	0

    £122 11 4

I have given an account of (55) in Chap. X. p. 65. (56) was son of Anthony Wade of King Cross, who had married Judith Foxcroft of New Grange, near Leeds. (57) was Vicar of Bradford from 1615 to 1639. His name is generally spelled Okell; he was uncle to Daniel Barraclough of Halifax, whose will is given in L.P.LIX. (58) was probably one of the "four learned preachers" sons of Richard Nichol of Southowram (P.R. under 1603). There are three additional subscriptions mentioned besides the above, amounting to £1 16 8, so that the sum total is £196 14 8, which exceeds the statement in the paragraph preceding the Lists. The Lists are signed by Jo: Farrer, Antony Foxcroft, Nathaniell Waterhouse, Thos: Lister, Edw. Hanson, John Drake.

CHAPTER XVII.

IT is of great advantage to a provincial school to have exhibitions or scholarships attached to it. The schools of York, Shrewsbury, Manchester, and Birmingham, for instance, have been able to send many scholars to the Universities, who have gained great honour for their schools, and have obtained by their ability high positions in the world. Fifty pounds per annum will not of course pay the expenses incurred at the Universities, but will be a considerable assistance to parents who are desirous of sending their sons there. Scholarships supply a stimulus to the scholars, and very few who gain them fail in obtaining additional pecuniary advantages, which enable them to go through the University Course without much burden to their parents. Birmingham School for instance has not only produced many men who took high degrees and are occupying useful positions in the world, but can reckon among its alumni the Bishops of Durham and Truro, and Canon Westcott, who were its exhibitioners. And many have left their mark on the history of the country, who owed their all to similar support. But at Heath School there is nothing of the kind. It has certainly an interest in some scholarships, but it has to compete with other schools, so that a parent can never reckon on any help as certain, however able his son may be, and those who have contributed any honour to the School by taking University Honours have done so without its assistance. Learning with an empty pocket cannot expect to succeed, and there is here no encouragement to men of slender means to send their sons, however talented, to a University. It is worth notice that the exhibitions at the schools which I have mentioned are due to the liberality of men who lived two or three centuries ago, and the present generation which feels a pride in the successes of those schools does so without having itself contributed anything towards them.

I have said that Heath School has some interest in exhibitions or scholarships, and I will now give some account of them; but I may say, Has no one any wish to raise the status of the School by adding to them? It should always be borne in mind that the School was not made for itself, but to prepare its scholars for something that was beyond it. Its education at the best was not intended to be final, but only preparatory for a higher stage.

Let us see what has been done with a view to this. John Milner, a native of Skircoat, and a scholar of Heath School, successively Vicar of St. John's Church in Leeds, and of the Parish Church there, had an only son, Thomas, who became Vicar of Bexhill in Suffolk. This son bequeathed in 1721 a sum of money to Magdalene College at Cambridge, to provide Scholarships for scholars from Heversham School in Westmorland, and from the schools of Leeds and Halifax. I am informed that these are now of the value of £80 a year. They are given, as they become vacant, to such candidates as successfully pass a prescribed examination which takes place every year in April. The Tutor of the College tells me that the subjects are :—" Euclid, Algebra, Trigonometry, Conic Sections, Passages from Greek and Latin Authors for Translation, and Composition in Greek and Latin Prose and Verse ". He also says :—" Preference will in general be given to excellence in one line of study ; but no one will be elected who does not satisfy the Examiners in the elementary parts of both Classics and Mathematics ".

There is another chance for the School. Some land was bequeathed in 1518* by William Akroyd, Rector of Long Marston, a priest of the pre-reformation Church, for the support of a scholar at Oxford or Cambridge. In consequence of an increase in its value there are now two open Scholarships, each of the annual value of £75, tenable at either University. There is an examination for these, when vacant, "in Classics, Mathematics, History, Geography, and one modern foreign language". Candidates are admitted "from any Endowed Schools in the County of York"; and consequently Heath School can send candidates.

In the spring of the present year, the Provost of Queen's College, Oxford, informed me that some of the twelve schools of Yorkshire, which had the privilege of sending candidates for Lady Betty Hastings' Exhibitions at that College, worth £90 a year, had forfeited their privilege, and he enquired what prospect there was of Heath School being able to send candidates. As there were no pupils sufficiently advanced at the time, he finally wrote:—"It will probably be your best plan to postpone your application to have the Heath School added to the Hastings Schools till your candidate is ready to offer himself. The Schools have only twenty years probation, and in case he should for any reason fail to appear, you might perhaps waste four or five years out of the twenty without having a candidate to send up".

With these three possibilities, the School requires only the support of those who wish to give their sons a University education; for if it has been able to train under the present management a Senior Classic, a Milner Scholar, and at least two others who have gained Scholarships in their respective Colleges, it is within its power to add to those Honours. But a good result cannot be expected, unless good material is supplied.

---

* An English translation of the Will is given in L.P. CLXII.

143

THE PRESENT PROSPECTUS OF THE SCHOOL.

Head Master - - REV. THOMAS COX, M.A., Camb*.
Master of Junior Department MR. J. CLAYTON, B.A., Camb.
Mathematical Master - MR. W. E. SADD, B.A., Camb.
French - - - - - MONSIEUR POIRE.
Drawing - MR. W. H. STOPFORD, of the School of Art.
Drill - - MR. T. MORLEY, late Sergeant-Major in the
Royal Artillery.

This School is managed under the Scheme drawn up by
the Endowed Schools Commissioners, and is divided into a
Senior and a Junior Department. No boy is admitted until
he is eight years old. He cannot remain in the Junior
Department beyond the end of the Term in which he attains
the age of FOURTEEN years; nor in the Senior Department
beyond the end of the Term in which he attains the age
of NINETEEN.

No boy can be admitted without undergoing an examination
by the Head Master, which in the Junior Department is
never to fall below the following standard :—*Reading easy
narrative: Writing small text-hand: Simple sums in the first
four rules of Arithmetic.* The Examination for admission to
the Senior Department is never to fall below the following
standard :—*Reading ordinary narrative: Writing simple prose
from dictation: Sums in the four simple and compound rules
of Arithmetic: English Grammar, Geography, Outlines of English
History: Latin Grammar, Translation and Parsing of simple
Latin sentences.*

In the Senior Department the education is more professional
than in the Junior, and includes Greek and the higher
branches of Mathematics.

All boys must learn French, except those in the lowest
class who are under TWELVE years of age. All must learn
Drawing in the Junior Department, except in the lowest

class, where it is optional. It is also optional at present in the Senior Department.

The religious education consists of the Bible History. Boys also receive instruction in the Book of Common Prayer, *or* the Psalms and Proverbs, at the option of their Parent or Guardian.

The Fees are (at present) £8 per annum for the Junior Department, and £12 per annum for the Senior. They are payable before the beginning of each Term to the Governors' Clerks, Messrs. Emmet & Walker, Harrison Road. *Notice of removal of a boy is to be given to the Head Master one month before the end of a Term, or the Fee will be charged for the next Term.*

There are THREE Terms in the year, the Lent Term beginning about January 14th; the Midsummer Term about April 14th; and the Michaelmas Term about September 14th.

The fixed holidays are FOUR WEEKS at Christmas, FOUR DAYS at Easter, TWO WEEKS at Whitsuntide, and SIX WEEKS at the end of the Midsummer Term.

There is an annual examination in July, conducted by a Graduate of one of the Universities.

The School hours are from 9 to 12, and from 2 to 5, except on Wednesday and Saturday, when there is a half-holiday. Every boy must be punctual and regular in attendance; and after absence he must bring a note signed by his Parent or Guardian, stating the cause. It is necessary for the welfare of the School that these points should be attended to. Every boy is expected to make up all deficiencies in school-work occasioned by such absence.

For convenience sake the books in use can be obtained from the Head Master.

* Mr. Cox took Honours both in Classics and Mathematics, being in the First Class in the former, and in the Second in the latter. Mr. Clayton and Mr. Sadd took Mathematical Honours, both being high in the Second Class. All three were Scholars or Exhibitioners of their respective Colleges. M. Poiré was specially trained as a teacher of English at the Training School of Cluny (Saône et Loire).

CORRECTIONS AND ADDITIONS.

p. 3, *note**. Brinsley was Master of the Ashby-de-la-Zouch Grammar School from 1601 to 1618. There is a good Article in Fraser's Magazine for November 1879, on what was taught in Grammar Schools in his day. The Article is an Enquiry into what Shakespeare learned at School.

p, 5. *l.* 21. I have generally left names spelled as I found them in documents. But here I should have written *Ashburne,* as I have done later on, when I lighted on his marriage register, in which it is spelled with *e*. *Farrar* sometimes has *a*, sometimes *e*, in the last syllable; and I have been in doubt which to adopt.

p. 10, *note* †. After *letters* insert *are*.

p. 14, *note **. For ' MSS.' read ' MS.'

p. 15, *l.* 29. For *time* read *live*.

p. 22, *l.* 5. In 1765 Gilbert Wakefield went at nine years of age to Wilford School near Nottingham. In his "Life", p. 29, he says:—"We came into the school at *five* in the summer, and, with the deduction of less than *two* hours intermission at *breakfast* and *dinner,* continued there till *six* at night".

p. 24, *l.* 21. Here is one of Brearcliffe's mistakes. He has copied P.R. wrongly.

p. 28, *l.* 20. Insert a comma after *School.*

p. 29, *l.* 7. Erase the comma after *known.*

p. 30, *note.* *i.e.,* "Samuel son of John Stancliffe, Southowram".

p. 31, *note* † For *ǝ* read *e*.

p. 32, *note ** R. Sterne's brother Roger, father of Laurence, is said to have been "somewhat rapid and hasty" in temper.

p. 34, *l.* 7. For *Haytor* read *Hayter*. I was long puzzled by the statement that Dr. Hayter, afterwards Bishop of Norwich, had drawn up the Statutes, until I found that he was at the time Secretary of the Archbishop of York.

„ *note* * *l.* 7. It is in the letter *Eleana*, a clerical error for *Elkanah*.

p. 38, *l.* 2. For *Stern* read *Sterne*.

p. 46, *l.* 23. *Chemistry* is not mentioned in the Scheme: but rooms have been provided for it in the New Building. The Governors have also outstripped the Scheme in building a Gymnasium.

p. 52, *note* 8. I had interpreted the cipher as "aprove," *i.e.*, "approve", but I did not know that the word was ever so applied. I have since found "prove" used technically in a similar way, and I would now read it as "approve".

p. 53, *note* 10*a*. It is also provided in the Statutes of Rotherham (1584), that Hesiod should be taught. I suppose it to be owing to the moral teaching of his principal poem.

„ *note* 11. The "book published in 1612" is Brinsley's *Ludus* to which I have referred before.

p. 55, *l.* 20. After *have* insert *been*.

p. 59, *note**. Add "cunning in knowledge, and understanding science. Daniel i, 4". There are many other instances in the Bible.

p. 61, *l.* 11. *xpo i.e.*, Christo, X in Greek being represented by Ch, and the character for *r* being almost like *p*.

„ *l.* 20. for *u* in *Richardu* read *ū i.e.*, *um*.

p. 66, *l.* 25. Timothy Booth was the father of R. Sterne's second wife.

p. 71, *l.* 29. The celebrated Dr. Johnson thought highly of Dr. Ogden's Sermons, especially those on prayer, as Boswell tells us, in describing his visit to Scotland, to which the Sermons had found their way.

p. 76, *l.* 5. The chair was taken by Col. Norcliffe of Langton Hall, near Malton: about 50 old pupils were present, as well as the Governors of the School.

„ *l.* 29. P.C. stand for "ponendum curaverunt".

„ *l.* 35. There are many anecdotes afloat respecting Mr. Wilkinson, but they are all too trifling to be given in this work.

p. 82, *l.* 16. I have found in Mr. Gooch's register the following names of Assistant Masters :—1854 Mr. Cranmer; 1855 Mr. Hiron, and Mr. Hadath; 1856 Mr. Morgan; 1858 Mr. Thwaite; 1859 Mr. Bissell, and Mr. James; 1860 Mr. T. Pitts. Since that date there have been 1861 Mr. J. C. Cammack; 1863 Mr. W. J. Brookes; 1865 Mr. Mead; 1869 Mr. H. J. Geare, and Mr. S. Jeffery; 1871 Mr. A. H. Chesshire; 1872 Mr. H. Sayers; 1874 Mr. F. H. Weston; and 1875 Mr. G. F. Blatch.

p. 84, *l.* 12. After *produced* insert a comma.

„ *l.* 16. On reference to the Cambridge Calendar, I find in 1760 "Joah Bates, Christ's" elected to the Craven Scholarship, the highest Classical Prize in the University. A note says, "Afterwards Fellow of King's, and conductor of the Commemoration of Handel in Westminster Abbey". Henry Bates was *fourth* Wrangler in 1759, and Members' Prizeman in 1761.

p. 90, *l.* 25. Late Lieutenant Colonel.

148

p. 91.   I have also received the following names of pupils
    of Mr. Wilkinson :—

1815	Crossley, David	182 .	Ramsden, John	
,,	Frobisher, —	,,	,,	William
1817	Bowerbank,—	,,	,,	George
,,	Fawthrop*,—	183 .	Slater, Abraham	
1819	Dyson, Frank	,,	,,	William
(?)	Wright, Joe	1832	Ashworth*, George Wheelhouse	
1821	Crossley, Harry	1833	Atkinson, Christopher	
,,	Jessop, —	,,	,,	Henry

p. 99, *l.* 1.   Child, H. E. A. entered in *January* 1872.

p. 100.   After the names add :—"Mr. Gooch admitted 349
    boys, an average of 18 per annum ; Mr. Cox admitted
    360, an average of 19 per annum ". It is singular
    that the Commissioners in 1827 give the average
    number of boys not boarders as 35, and the Governors
    in 1861 give the same average. My average up to
    1875 was 42, and during the last 5 years has been
    about the same. I have not taken account of boarders
    or of my own sons.

p. 103, *l.* 21.   Add the remarks of W. Bagehot on this :—
    "But 'genius' is rarely popular in places of education ;
    and it is, to say the least, remarkable that so
    sentimental a man as Sterne should have chanced
    upon so sentimental an instructor. It is wise to be
    suspicious of aged reminiscents ; they are like persons
    entrusted with 'untold gold' ; there is no check on
    what they tell us. *Literary Studies, ii.* 108.

p. 109, *l.* 10.   After *was* put a comma.

p. 110, *l.* 10.   For *similiar* read *similar*.

p. 111, *l.* 25.   This Tablet was presented by Mr. Cox in 1870.

    „   *note*   For '1706' read '1796'.

p. 115, *l.* 8.   For MS. read MSS.

FINIS.

149

(ADDITIONAL)

CORRECTED LIST OF THE GOVERNORS, JANUARY, 1880.

(drawn up since the body of the work was printed).

EX-OFFICIO.
{ Matthew Smith (Alderman) — *Mayor.*
{ John Henry Swallow — *Chairman of School Board.*

REPRESENTATIVE.

⌠ Samuel Thomas Midgley (Alderman)
| John William Longbottom (Alderman) ⎫
| Nathan Whitley ⎬ *Elected by Town Council,* 1879.
| John Hall (Councillor) ⎭
|
| John Edwards Hill ⎫
| Alfred Ramsden (Councillor) ⎬ *Elected by School Board,* 1879.
| William Morris — *Bairstow's Charity, Sowerby.*
⌡ John Farrar — *Brooksbank's Charity, Elland.*

CO-OPTATIVE.

⌠ Edward Rawson
| Henry Edwards (Bart)
| Samuel Waterhouse (Major)
⎨ William Henry Rawson *(President Governor).*
| Edward Akroyd (Col.)
| William Rothwell
| Joshua Appleyard
⌡ John Rawson

p. 131, *l.* 17. For 'Worcestor' read 'Worcester'.

p. 132, *note†* For 'L.L.D' read 'LL.D'.

P.S.—The writer of this work is sorry that there has been so long a delay in publication. He could have brought it out some months ago, had it not been for the Illustrations, which have taken a longer time than was expected.

Jan. 31, 1880.